Rethinking the Rules of Financial Accounting

Examining the Rules for Proper Reporting

Robert N. Anthony

McGraw-Hill

New York   Chicago   San Francisco   Lisbon   London   Madrid
Mexico City   Milan   New Delhi   San Juan   Seoul
Singapore   Sydney   Toronto

The *McGraw·Hill* Companies

1 2 3 4 5 6 7 8 9 0   AGM/AGM   0 9 8 7 6 5 4 3

ISBN 0-07-142387-7

This book is printed on recycled, acid-free paper containing a minimum of 50% recycled de-inked paper.

Library of Congress Cataloging-in-Publication Data

Anthony, Robert Newton, 1916-
    Rethinking the rules of financial accounting : examining the rules for proper financial reporting / by Robert N. Anthony.
        p. cm.
    ISBN 0-07-142387-7 (hardcover : alk. paper)
    1. Accounting. 2. Financial statements. I. Title.
    HF5635. A715 2003
    657'.3—dc21
                                                                    2003004809

CONTENTS

Acknowledgments

Two are outstanding. Betty Waterman, for her memory, her writing skill, and her ability to improve on my words in a polite way. The book would not have existed without her. Susan Newberry, who has commented on my work for many years with insight and knowledge.

Anita Warren did an excellent job of editing. Stefanie Bernstein was my researcher.

Co-authors of books

(Harvard Business School unless otherwise indicated)

Leslie Pearlman Breitner, University of Washington; D.C. Dearborn; John Dearden; Patricia P. Douglas, Montana State University; Vijay Govindarajan, Tuck School; David Hawkins; James S. Hekiman; Regina Herzlinger; Kenneth Merchant, University of Southern California; Jim Reece, The University of Michigan; Samuel Schwartz; H. David Sherman; J. S. Sinclair, Bentley School; Richard V. Vancil; David Young, Boston University.

Others

Charles A. Anderson; Dennis R. Beresford, University of Georgia; Sarah J. Buckingham, Tuck School Library, Dartmouth College; Mary Fischer, University of Texas at Tyler; Neil Harlan; D. Eric Hirst, University of Texas at Austin; Martin Ives; Lawrence R. Jones, The Naval Postgraduate School; Donald J. Kirk, Columbia University; Leornard Marks, Jr.; James G. Roche, Secretary of the Air Force; Sheila Weinberg, Congressional Committee Staff member; Stephen A. Zeff, Rice University.

1

INTRODUCTION

Financial accounting statements are documents that provide outside parties with financial information about the historical performance and current status of an organization. Until fairly recently there were no published rules regarding principles, standards, and procedures for financial accounting statements. Organizations are expected to follow the established rules to assure an acceptable picture of an organization's financial status. Users of financial statements—managers, lenders, government bodies, and investors—have a right to expect that the numbers in a financial document will correspond to a sensible set of rules. Therefore, users of financial statements must rely on a rule-setting body to create authoritative, sensible regulations for preparing financial statements.

Currently, there are four sets of authoritative rules in the United States:

1. Rules for business organizations established by the Financial Accounting Standards Board (FASB). These rules are subject to approval by the Securities and Exchange Commission.
2. Rules for nonprofit organizations established by the FASB.
3. Rules for state and local government accounting established by the Governmental Accounting Standards Board (GASB).

4. Rules for the federal government established by the Federal Accounting Standards Advisory Board (FASAB), although there is
   some doubt about whether these rules are authoritative.

If the financial statement of an organization does not follow
all these rules and if the defect is material, the statement receives a "qualified opinion" from its auditor. If the organization is listed on the Securities and Exchange Commission, the
commission will suspend trading immediately. In other organizations a qualified opinion usually results in nonaccep-
tance of the statement. Qualified opinions are rare.

The last reexamination of these rules occurred in the 1970s.
Two committees of the American Institute of Certified Public
Accountants (AICPA)—the Wheat Committee (1971) and the
Trueblood Committee (1973)—laid the groundwork for the
creation of the FASB.

The rules of the FASB and the GASB, totaling over 2,000
pages of text, are in general excellent; however, some of those
rules are defective. In this book I focus on the defective rules
and suggest ways to cure the defects. The suggestions are
limited to financial accounting rules; they do not deal with
rules governing the behavior of the accountants or auditors
who use the rules. Ethical behavior cannot be specified in
rules; therefore, my suggestions do not deal with ethical concepts.

Focus

The four sets of rules established by the FASB, GASB, and
FASAB share the following basic characteristics:

1. The amounts are monetary.
2. The amounts are consistent with a basic structure that includes the equation assets = liabilities + equity. (Some struc-
   tures use different names.) The structure also satisfies the
   equation debits = credits.

3. There are two principal types of financial statements. The first, usually referred to as a balance sheet, reports the financial status of an organization at the end of an accounting period, usually one year. The second, often called an income statement, reports changes in equity or some subdivision of equity within an accounting period.

It is these three characteristics that are important to my discussion of the defective rules and the solutions to resolving the defects.

Limitations on Focus

This book does not deal with the following topics:

- Notes to the financial statements. These notes amplify or explain the rules and may contain nonmonetary information.
- Rules for conducting audits.
- Nonmonetary rules for performance measurement. The rules often are referred to as the balanced scorecard. If they are not derived from the financial accounting system, they are not financial accounting information.
- Ratios and other summary numbers derived from financial statements. Some people propose that the rules should contain formulas for performance measurement; I do not discuss these possibilities.
- Information in the published accounting standards that are not rules. This information may describe the rule-making process, the organization's environment, or other information not required to arrive at acceptable accounting financial statement numbers.
- Rules by a body that has no enforcement power. The standards of the Internal Federation of Accountants (IFAC) are an example.
- Rules of the International Accounting Standards Board (IASB). However, these rules are generally consistent with the

ones I discuss. The FASB has made important steps toward merging its rules with those of the IFAC. Eventually there should be a single set of financial accounting rules for all developed countries.

- Rules set by industry associations. These rules are not authoritative.
- Rules recently established by the FASB for revenue recognition, definition of an asset, consolidated financial statements, business combinations, accounting for "fresh starts," and certain types of financial instruments. These rules were adopted after an excellent discussion of the issues, and it would be premature to suggest that any of them are defective until several years have elapsed.

The rules of the FASAB are inconsistent with the rules stated by other bodies. The FASAB rules are discussed as a separate topic in Chapter 10.

Background

Reports of an organization's monetary standing go back to the fourth century B.C. Rules for information reported to regulatory agencies, tax collectors, and other government bodies have been in existence ever since that time. It was not until the twentieth century that the United States developed and implemented rules for the preparation of financial statements by businesses and other organizations. Until 1938 there was no American rule-making body, and accountants relied on texts and articles for guidance. Public accounting firms began to develop their own rules, some of which were published. *Montgomery's Auditing*, for example, had considerable acceptance among accountants even though it was not issued by an authoritative body and therefore could not be truly authoritative. In litigation, accounting experts relied on these published sources and on the decisions of trial courts, appellate courts, and even the U.S. Supreme Court.

There were many differences of opinion about how accounting transactions should be booked. In litigation, the plaintiff's expert witness would cite practices described by respected authors and in legal precedents. The defendant's witness would cite evidence from another source that supported the opposite position. That testimony relied on the opinions of both federal and state courts. The experts' assistants would spend many hours searching case records for decisions that would support the desired interpretation. The objective of that research was to identify "generally accepted accounting principles," but "generally accepted," as used in litigation, meant acceptance by individual experts or by a few respected companies that practiced those principles. Their "acceptance" was not always "general."

Committee on Accounting Procedures

The first official rule-making body in the United States was AICPA's Committee on Accounting Procedures.[1] Working with only a small staff, the committee's members were public accountants and academics who served part-time. In 1938 the AICPA authorized this committee to issue pronouncements stating what its members judged to be "generally accepted" principles. Those opinions were restated and revised in *Accounting Research Bulletin (ARB)* No. 43, issued in 1953. ARB 43 stated that "the authority of opinions reached by the committee rests upon their general acceptability."

Accounting Principles Board

In 1958 the AICPA created the Accounting Principles Board (APB) and charged it with developing rules for financial accounting. The APB had the same basic weakness as its predecessor: The members were part-time, and the staff was small.

The APB pronouncements were the first authoritative pronouncements; that is, an auditor could not give a "clean" audit opinion on financial statements that departed from those rules in any material respect. An auditor who gave a clean opinion to a financial statement that had a material defect was subject to sanctions by the AICPA and possibly to a lawsuit.

In the 15 years of its existence the APB issued 31 opinions; however, 10 were superseded by other opinions, leaving a total of 21 topics.

Two of the board's members—Maurice Moonitz and Bob Sprouse—developed a much-needed document: *A Tentative Set of Principles for Business Enterprises* (AICPA Research Study No. 3). The APB did not adopt that report, however, stating that its principles were "too radically different from present generally accepted accounting principles for acceptance at this time."

Financial Accounting Standards Board

The FASB began functioning in 1973 and issued its first standard in that year. By 2002 it had issued six concepts (CON) statements[2] and 146 standards.

The FASB has seven full-time members and, currently, a staff of about 40. It derives its authority from the Financial Accounting Foundation (FAF), which was created by the AICPA. The FAF receives funds from contributions and obtains revenues from sales of its publications. Theoretically, it has "oversight" responsibility for the standards-setting process, but as a practical matter this function has been limited to a fairly general annual report.

The FASB also publishes the recommendations of its Emerging Issues Task Force. Those recommendations are authoritative, but they appear in a publication separate from the FASB standards. Although conclusions of the task force should be incorporated in those standards, this has not happened. They are the task force's conclusions on certain specific specialized issues.

Unlike many other standards-setting bodies, especially the IASB, the FASB has never conducted an overall review of its standards. In the last decade there have been several reports that expressed dissatisfaction with the standards and recommended drastic changes in the underlying concepts. Those reports are listed in the next section.

The creation of the FASB resulted in a new and most likely inevitable problem: a decline in the number of published articles on accounting standards.[3] Most people with new ideas recognized that since the FASB calls the shots, publishing an article in a journal probably would be a waste of effort. Many letters to the FASB criticized existing standards or proposed new standards. The FASB refers to some of these letters in the Basis for Conclusions section of its pronouncements. Since that section was intended to support the FASB's rules, articles that are inconsistent with them are glossed over.

The FASB files are open to public inspection. However, the summaries, which are created by FASB staff members, abridging the comments on exposure drafts, are not made available to the public. Individuals can prepare their own summaries of those letters, but this rarely happens because the process is so time-consuming. I participated in developing a summary of the 1,193 letters responding to the exposure draft that became Financial Accounting Standard (FAS) 93. That exposure draft proposed that long-lived assets be depreciated in nonprofit entities. Although 92 percent of the letters argued against the proposed standard, they did not persuade the FASB to change the exposure draft. In FAS99 the FASB delayed the date of the original implementation of FAS93 for two years, and it later rejected a formal request to reconsider it. FAS 93 did not state that its position differed from that of a huge majority of letters.

The analysis of depreciation dealt with a specific, easy-to-analyze issue. The task would be much more demanding for complicated issues.

International Accounting Standards Board

The International Accounting Standards Committee (IASC), which was formed in 1973, develops worldwide accounting standards. The IASC was reorganized as the IASB in 2001. Currently consisting of 14 members, 12 of whom are full-time, its membership organization (similar to the Financial Accounting Foundation) has representatives from over 100 countries.

The IASB standards were revised in the 1990s on the basis of an examination similar to the one I will recommend in this book. Those standards are in most respects consistent with FASB standards, but they make their point in fewer words. Efforts are under way to eliminate the few substantial differences between the IASB rules and the FASB rules; this will require compromise from each body.

Securities and Exchange Commission

The U.S. Securities and Exchange Commission (SEC) was established in 1934 in response to the collapse of banking and stock exchanges. It is responsible for monitoring the financial information issued by all the 17,000 companies listed on a stock exchange. The organization's five members are appointed by the President, and the accounting rules it publishes in SEC Regulation SX have the force of law. The chief accountant of the SEC or his or her representative serves on many FASB committees. The SEC has stated that it would rely on rules issued by the FASB unless those rules were judged to be unsound. The commission has differed from the FASB on a few issues and has published rules that are inconsistent with those of the FASB.

Each year the SEC identifies 400 to 500 civil enforcement actions against individuals and companies that did not conform to the rules. Most of those actions have been related to minor violations of the rules; however, a few have been substantial.

In 2001 Arthur Andersen agreed to pay a fine of $7 million to settle a case brought by the SEC which charged the firm with fraud related to audits of Waste Management. The fines imposed on Andersen partners individually totaled $120,000, and those partners will be barred from practicing for public companies for a period of one to five years.

Occasionally an accounting firm may insist that the client has not followed generally accepted accounting principles (GAAP), and the difference comes to public attention. For example, XEROX Corporation publicly dismissed its audit firm KPMG LLP after KPMG wrote a report criticizing XEROX's accounting practices (*Wall Street Journal*, October 8, 2001).

Recent Developments

Currently there is much dissatisfaction with the state of business financial accounting standards. Critics include Dennis R. Beresford, former FASB chair,[4] Arthur Levitt, former chair of the SEC;[5] Samuel A. Derieux, former chair of the AICPA;[6] and John Reed, chief executive officer (CEO) of Citicorp and chair of the influential Business Roundtable.[7] Van Riper wrote an excellent description of the growing dissatisfaction.[8]

AICPA Action

In 1994 the AICPA Special Committee on Financial Reporting issued a 200-page report titled *Improving Business Reporting— A Customer Focus: Meeting the Information Needs of Investors and Creditors*. In 1996 the AICPA held a symposium of representatives of accounting organizations to discuss ways to implement the recommendations in that report, but no such action has been published. A 1997 article in the *Journal of Accountancy* concluded, "Practically all symposium participants favored forming a coalition to develop best reporting practices . . . FASB should be the leader."[9] This also has not happened.

The Financial Accounting Standards Advisory Council

The Financial Accounting Standards Advisory Council is a component of the FAF. It issues an annual report listing topics that need to be reconsidered, but the topics discussed in those reports are trivial. Few of them have led to action by the FASB.

XBRL Project

A large committee is developing terminology and procedures that may govern financial accounting statements posted on the Internet. This committee was organized under the auspices of the AICPA, but it is now an independent group that is financed by its member organizations. The members include accountants from large firms, computer experts from major software companies, and academics. This accounting system is discussed in Chapter 2.

The Association for Investment Management and Research

In 1993 the Association for Investment Management and Research (AIMR), which is the principal association of investment analysts, issued a critical report titled *Financial Reporting in the 1990s and Beyond*. That report criticized a large number of the current accounting rules. The FASB has done little about its recommendations.

Other Business Reports

Recently, there have been at least eight reports recommending drastic changes in accounting concepts and standards. The most important ones are *Performance Measures in the New Economy* (Toronto, 1995), Robert I. G. McLean, Canadian Institute of Chartered Accountants; *Improving Business Reporting:*

Insights into Enhancing Voluntary Disclosures (1998), FASB
Steering Committee, Business Reporting Research Project; *The
GAAP Gap: Corporate Disclosure in the Internet Age* (March
2000), Brookings Institution and American Enterprise Institute; *New Measures for the New Economy* (2000), Charles Lead-
better, Institute of Chartered Accountants in England and
Wales; and *Strengthening Financial Markets: Do Investors Have
the Information They Need?* (May 2001), SEC.

The general theme of several of those reports is that the important information in accounting has shifted from tangible
assets (e.g., buildings and equipment) to intangible assets
(e.g., goodwill, investment instruments). As stated in the excellent Special Report by Wayne S. Upton, Jr., of the FASB, the
central message of these reports is that "the economy of 2000
is fundamentally different from the economy of the 1950s
and . . . traditional financial statements do not capture—and
may not be able to capture—the value drivers that dominate
the new economy." Upton lists some of the proposed measurements, including customer focus, human focus, process
focus, and renewal and development focus. It seems highly
unlikely, however, that these measurements could be included in the financial accounting system (i.e., debits equals
credits), as it would be difficult to assign a financial value to
these intangibles. The problem is that there is no way to measure the value of information (patents, research and development in process, etc.).

Upton could not find any references to the widespread use
of any particular measurement system, and neither can I.
Rather, individual companies are using their own systems for
their own needs.

Baruch Lev and Paul Zarowin.   "The Boundaries of Financial
Reporting and How to Extend Them" by Baruch Lev and Paul
Zarowin demonstrates that increasing defects in financial
accounting reports have been associated with increasing
differences between accounting information and companies'
actual performance and status in the period 1978–1996.[10]

Those authors indicated that there is declining usefulness in accounting information on earnings. Those differences are caused by the inability of accounting to report the actual effect of research and development (R&D) expenditures, restructuring, and deregulation. The authors recommend capitalizing R&D expenditures when there is a "working model of software or a clinical test of a drug" and also recommend that past financial statements be restated when there is adequate evidence that the effect of these changes was to increase profits.

Adopting these recommendations may improve the usefulness of accounting information, but at the risk of increased "earnings management." The recommendations do not solve the basic problem: the fact that the effect of changes inevitably is uncertain. A technically successful new product may not in fact result in additional profits.

Some of these recommendations are fundamentally new names for old ideas. For example, "entity resource planning" was described in textbooks under other titles many years ago.

Pro-Forma Earnings.   One of the topics under consideration is "pro-forma earnings." This term refers to income statements that are not consistent with GAAP but include numbers that management states are a better measure of performance than those required. This technique is used by many companies in the management discussion analysis section of financial statements. Although many young companies believe that pro-forma earnings information should be published, doing so would negate one of the basic premises of financial accounting, the premise that revenues are not included in a statement if they do not refer to goods or services that have been delivered to customers.

A study of 233 companies by National Investor Relations Institute (NIRI) reported that 133 companies reported pro-forma information with prominence. The SEC understandably does not like this development, which implies erroneously that pro-forma earnings are acceptable accounting numbers. It has instituted cease-and-desist proceedings against Trump Hotels & Casino Resorts Inc., which reported pro-forma information.[11]

Congress

Recently Congress passed the Sarbanes-Oxley Act of 2002, which contains many generalities but few specific ways to correct the auditing situation. As Warren Buffett said, "Indeed, actions by Congress and the Securities and Exchange Commission have the potential of creating a smoke screen that will prevent real accounting reform."[12]

In the discussion leading to the Sarbanes-Oxley Act of 2002 there was much discussion of the treatment of stock options. In the final conference there was agreement with the concept that stock options result in expenses, but there was no agreement about how this expense should be measured. Therefore, the topic did not appear in the law.

In the discussions leading to the law, there was also disagreement on the treatment of what are called Special Purposes Entities (SPEs). SPEs are organizations, usually partnerships, that are set up to accept liabilities for another organization but do not show up in the balance sheet of the consolidated corporation. This practice was not discussed in the Sarbanes-Oxley Act of 2002. It was, however, dealt with in an exposure draft of the FASB dated August 30, 2002.

Bubbles

History provides a number of examples of unwise investment decisions. Many have resulted in a pseudoprosperity, with future estimates placing too much emphasis on the probable profitability of certain organizations.[13]

The first mania was the tulip mania:

"In 1611, the world's first stock market was inaugurated in a specially created building in the heart of Amsterdam. The first crash occurred only 25 years after the inauguration! A tulip mania began in 1625 in Holland as tulips became to be considered an investment by the population. By 1634, the rage for owning tulips had spread to the middle classes of the Dutch society. The value of a tulip bulb grew from 5 florins in 1625 to as much as 5500 florins by 1636."

"In 1636, some began to liquidate their tulip holdings. Tulip prices began to weaken, slowly at first, and then rapidly. Confidence was soon destroyed, and panic seized the market. Within six weeks, tulip prices crashed by 90 percent!"[14]

After the boom in the early years of the twentieth century, the Panic of 1907 gave way to Progressive Era reforms, including the creation of the Federal Reserve System. In the early twentieth century Arthur Andersen was influential in introducing reforms in accounting standards. Then, as now, the United States was emerging from a successful war effort, in today's case the Cold War. In 1929 unwise investment decisions led to the bankruptcy of many banks and savings and loans associations, touching off the Depression. The president of the New York Stock Exchange was one of the culprits. The situation was mitigated by the passage of the Banking Act of 1933, which required federal deposit insurance and placed limits on how banks invest their funds. This and other restrictions are described in the Public Utility Holding Act of 1935 and the Investment Company Act of 1940.

In 1996 the 1940 Act was broadened to include more types of corporations and was especially useful to Enron. The 1940 Act originally was intended to aid banks, but more recently it was used by a few aggressive corporations. The device used was called special purpose entities. An SPE, as described above, is a limited partnership that makes the consolidated balance sheet ratios look much better than they would appear if the SPE data had been included in them. If things do not go right, the SPE organization can cause severe financial problems, and this was the principal reason for the bankruptcy of Enron Corporation.

Enron

A recent, large fiasco was that of the Enron Corporation, so named in 1986. Mergers and acquisitions by Enron started in the 1940s and continued through the year 2000. The conglomerate was incorporated in 1930 as Northern Natural Gas Company, and it remained in this single industry for many years. In February 1986 Kenneth Lay became chairman of the board, and the company immediately began a vast expansion. During the 1990s it fully acquired 62 new companies and partially acquired 55 more. Enron expanded into the energy and communication industries, including transportation and shipping, sanitary services, mining, photo equipment, clocks, business services, and water distribution. New countries were penetrated by the Enron name: China, Germany, Brazil, Argentina, the Netherlands, Australia, South Korea, Venezuela, Panama, Mexico, India, and Hungary. In *Fortune*'s list of innovative companies Enron was in the "highest scorers" category from 1996 through 1999. By 1997 ENRON was the eighth largest corporation in the United States. The numbers and diversity of those acquisitions made auditing the financial status of the company an impossible task, but there were other complications. Enron officials created a number of SPEs. In the typical SPE the liability of the partners is limited, but an Enron official promised that Enron would be liable for any of the SPEs' obligations.

The SPEs were not counted as Enron's subsidiaries and were not included in the financial statements. However, they were not legally liable to Enron Corporation for their debts.

Andrew Fastow, who was the chief financial officer and executive vice president, was responsible for many of these financing innovations. Fastow's personal income rose to $30 million as a result of the way he structured transactions related to acquisitions. Several other executives earned huge incomes as well.

Investors in Enron were impressed by the outlook, and the stock peaked at $90.75 in August 2000. In 2001 the bubble burst when the investment community suddenly decided that the Enron outlook was not sufficiently rosy to warrant that price. In August 2001 Enron's stock was at $34.58; in December of that year it hit rock bottom at 26 cents.

In most acquisitions the sales price is an accurate measure of the transaction. The acquiring company decides that the acquisition price is a fair amount to pay, and the acquired company already has decided that it is a fair amount to receive. However, in many Enron acquisitions the transactions did not meet these criteria, as subsequently became apparent. For example, Enron based its purchase price of Enron Energy Services on revenues that might be earned after the deregulation of electricity. In subsequent years the asset amount should be reduced to the then fair value, but Enron did not do this.

Enron could no longer meet its payments on outstanding liabilities, and the company filed for bankruptcy on December 2, 2001. Some analysts recommended Enron as a good investment shortly before this (Susanne Craig and Jonathan Weil, "Despite Losses, Complex Deals Analysts Remain high on ENRON," *Wall Street Journal*, October 26, 2001). Enron managers have also been indicted on several other violations of securities laws. The fact that certain Enron executives recommended that employees add Enron shares to their retirement portfolios at the same time they were cashing in Enron shares of their own indicates an ethical problem.

Although the Enron case was a fiasco, the accounting statements did eventually report what actually happened.

In the late 1990s there was "irrational exuberance," as Alan Greenspan referred to it, in the dot-com bubble period. Some companies were organized and sold stock with few or no real assets. Similar situations occurred at WorldCom, Qwest, Global Crossing, Tyco, and Adelphia. In addition to these overall culprits, the SEC uncovered large specific errors in the financial statements of a number of companies, including AOL, Imclone, Halliburton, Bristol-Myers Squibb Co., and Peregrine.

An interesting but perhaps irrelevant recent development is that according to fashion designers, business attire changed from suits, ties, and dresses to casual dress beginning in the 1980s.

Approach

The rules governing any measurement system are based on a set of concepts that provide overall guidance. In this review of financial accounting, I accept most of those concepts and focus on the standards that presumably are consistent with them. A few concepts that are controversial are described in Chapter 2.

Most disciplines—physics, chemistry, economics, medicine, engineering, and mathematics—have a conceptual framework for reporting measurements and a set of rules consistent with that framework. Those frameworks and rules have to be examined from time to time as the world changes. Inconsistencies in the rules creep in over time, and the rules do not incorporate new measurement techniques. Widespread dissatisfaction develops as a result. This book focuses on those rules which are in need of examination.

I do not provide an overall appraisal of the work of the FASB. On many topics the FASB has published sensible rules, many of which concern extremely complicated topics. There are a few not-so-sensible rules, and it is on those rules that I provide an overview.

Notes

[1] This committee was accompanied by the Committee on Terminology.
[2] The most recent concepts statement is called CON 7, but CON 3 became a

part of CON 6, and so there are only six separate statements. Concepts are intended to guide the development of accounting standards. Actually, they are used for this purpose only rarely.

[3] In *A History of Accountancy in the United States* (1998), Previts and Merino name 35 individuals who wrote important books or articles on accounting principles in the 26 years before the formation of the FASB and only 8 who did so in the 22 years after its formation. FASB members L. Todd Johnson and Robert J. Swieringa wrote an excellent article on board deliberations on accounting for financial instruments, but they do not make a single reference to concepts statements. There are 73 FASB statements on financial statements in business enterprises, but only 13 of them refer to CON 6, which presumably describes concepts relating to the elements of financial statements. See *Essays in Accounting Theory: A Capstone*, by Carl Thomas Devine, edited by Harvey Hendrickson (New York: Garland Publishing, 1999).

[4] Dennis R. Beresford, "It's Time to Simplify Accounting Standards," *Journal of Accountancy*, March 1999, pp. 65–67.

[5] As one of his several speeches, see Arthur Levitt, "Renewing the Covenant with Investors," given at the New York University Center for Law and Business, May 10, 2000.

[6] Samuel A. Derieux, "Let's Reassess Accounting Standards," *Journal of Accountancy*, May 2000, pp. 82–83.

[7] "Corporate America Is Fed Up with FASB," *Business Week*, April 21, 1997, p. 108.

[8] R. Van Riper, *Setting Standards for Financial Reporting*, Westport, CT: Quorum Books, 1994.

[9] Jerry J. Weygandt and Daniel J. Noll, "Business Reporting: What Comes Next," *Journal of Accountancy*, February 1997, p. 59.

[10] Unpublished manuscript.

[11] U.S. Securities and Exchange Commission press release, January 16, 2002.

[12] "Who Really Cooks the Books?" *New York Times*, July 24, 2002.

[13] See Charles P. Kindleberger, *Manias, Panics, and Crashes: A History of Financial Crises* (New York: Basic Books), 1978.

[14] Taken from a summary of an essay written by Nicholas Vendewalle, University of Liege, Belgium. Market Topology.Com, "Financial Crashes: Facts and Models."

2
CRITERIA

Accounting rules are rules for measurement. The definition of measurement is "the process of associating numbers with physical quantities and phenomena." Financial accounting rules measure "physical quantities" in three categories—assets, liabilities, and equity—at one moment in time. They measure "phenomena" as the quantities that change within an accounting period. Two types of changes affect equity: revenues and expenses.

All measurement processes contain rules that have general applicability. Those rules govern other rules, including the rules issued by government agencies. Examples are the weights and measures published by the U.S. Bureau of Weights and Measures. There is an international body: the International Organization for Standardization. Private bodies, such as industry associations, also set rules.

The details of any measurement system are governed by generalizations, definitions, principles, and what the Financial Accounting Standards Board (FASB) calls "concepts." A concept is a general idea, and rules are applications of concepts to specific situations. The rules, or standards, are supposed to conform to the concepts. The concepts do not govern the actual measurements directly, however. Many accounting concepts are not referred to in any accounting rule. Among the 476 paragraphs in the first five concepts statements, for example, only a third are referred to in standards.

In a few cases there may be conflicting concepts. An example is reporting a long-lived asset on the balance sheet after that asset has been acquired. The concept of "usefulness" requires that an asset be reported at its fair value, but the fair value may not be obtainable. The concept of "objectivity" requires that an asset be recorded at its acquisition cost or written off when it is purchased; these are the only available objective amounts. Accounting takes a middle ground by reporting the amount at cost less an allowance for depreciation. This practice, however, is neither entirely useful nor entirely objective.

The controversy over how to treat the exploratory drilling costs of oil and gas companies is another illustration of the difficulty of weighing different concepts. In the "successful efforts" method only the costs of wells discovered in the year reported should be capitalized; other costs incurred during that year should be expensed. By contrast, full cost advocates argue that *all* the drilling costs in a year should be capitalized and written off as expenses in the future years associated with revenue from the oil and gas produced. The FASB should clarify the matter by choosing one solution.

The FASB has not published a concise list of concepts and their definitions. Some of them are given in the FASB's concepts statements; others are not stated by the FASB because they are obvious to accountants.[1]

In this chapter I discuss (1) generally accepted rules for measurement, which are broader than rules for accounting, and (2) accounting concepts that govern accounting standards. The following material applies to measurement systems of all types, as is discussed below. I also mention concepts that are important in identifying accounting standards but do not analyze those concepts as such.

Measurements in General

This section lists criteria that are relevant to measurement systems in general. Financial accounting is one of those systems.

Unique Titles

The terms reported in the financial accounting system should be unique; that is, there should be only one name for each item. There should be no synonyms in the system.

A 2001 study by Bovee and associates provides an example of what happens when the criterion is not met. The study found that the balance sheets of the 67 firms listed in the EDGAR database (terms used by the Securities and Exchange Commission) listed accounts payable under a host of different titles, including trade accounts payable, accounts payable, accrued expenses, payables to affiliates, bank overdrafts, commercial paper, short-term notes payable, line of credit, short-term debt, loans current portion, debentures current portion, notes payable current portion, unsecured debt current portion, commercial paper current portion, notes and loans current portion, current portion of long-term debt, employee benefits, other employee-related liabilities, income tax payable, interest payable, and current liabilities.[2] This list should be reduced to a few terms that are subsets of accounts payable.

In 1998 I made a study of FASB concepts and standards that showed that often there were two names for the same item. For example, "operating income" was used 356 times and "operating profit" was used 146 times. Moreover, there was no stated definition of either term; the meaning had to be derived from the context, which can be subject to different interpretations. Some elements, such as cost, were not defined. "Cost" is an important and often misunderstood term. Resource outflows were called variously expenses, disbursements, spent, and costs. Each term has a different meaning, but those meanings were not made clear.

Terminology

The preferred terminology is that of the FASB, which is essentially the same as that of the International Accounting Standards Board (IASB). Difficulties in terminology result because those who developed nonprofit accounting rules and government rules used the terminology from their disciplines as a starting point rather than accepting the FASB rules.[3] This has led to much misunderstanding about the financial statements of nonbusiness organizations. For example, a nonprofit organization has a bottom line, which should be called "net income," exactly like that of a business company. The only difference between a business and a nonprofit organization is that a business obtains funds from investors whereas a nonprofit organization obtains funds from contributors or grantors.

Current pronouncements of rules for nonprofit organizations and government organizations use terms different from those used for businesses. This is unnecessary and confusing. The terminology for business amounts should determine when the term used means the same for a business and for a nonprofit.

The word "operating" is used often in FASB pronouncements, but the FASB has never defined it. This term should be defined. Some terms may be used by several industries but defined differently by each one.

There should be no synonyms. The bottom line on an income statement should be called "net income," not "net profit." "Earnings," which is not quite the same as "net income," should be defined separately, not used as another term for net income.

Taxonomy

The structure of the current FASB standards is chronological; that is, the standards are numbered, with more recent rules coming after earlier rules, for example, FAS 1, "Disclosure of Foreign Currency Translation Information" (1973), and FAS 2, "Accounting for Research and Development Costs" (1974).

In many other systems the elements of the reported statements are arranged in a hierarchy called a taxonomy. A taxonomy is a classification, especially in relation to its general laws or principles. It can be defined as the department of science or of a particular science or subject which consists in or relates to classification. The lowest terms are "elements." Elements are combined into "subcategories," subcategories into "categories," and categories into "sections" of the statement. Most of these terms can be subdivided further. For example, the hierarchy or kingdom of dogs has the following subitems: phylum, subphylum, superclass, class, subclass, infraclass, order, family, subfamily, genus, and species.

A body called the eXtensible Business Reporting Language (XBRL) Committee has been developing an accounting hierarchy. The committee has grown rapidly: At its meeting in Toronto in 2002 there were more than 160 representatives from over 80 of the world's leading accounting, technology, financial services, and government organizations. The committee accepts the labels now being used by individual companies, and the result has been more than 500 different taxonomies. It is reducing this number to 13 taxonomies. The work of the committee does not yet have authoritative support from the FASB, but it represents an excellent beginning to a financial accounting taxonomy. The individual labels have to be converted to a single name for each type of number.

The International Accounting Standards Committee Foundation (IASCF) has released the IASCF "Core" XBRL Taxonomy. Several countries are developing a taxonomy. This is unfortunate; there should be one taxonomy for the whole world.

The XBRL is a refinement of the basic idea of a chart of accounts. However, instead of having the account numbers derived by each company, all companies will use the numbers in the first several fields. XBRL has described the computer language that should be used for financial statements. If all companies used the same titles, the advantages in understanding balance sheets and preparing ratios or other data from individual companies would be tremendous.

Suggested changes in this taxonomy are described in Chapter 9.

Conciseness

Each term should be defined, perhaps with examples of its meaning, but that is all. An explanation of how a definition was determined should appear only in an appendix. Other material is irrelevant and distracts from the point being made.

Concepts Statement 2, "Qualitative Characteristics of Accounting Information," is the best-written concepts statement of all, but there is no need for its 144 paragraphs describing the five qualities and the relationships among them. Actually, there are only three "qualitative characteristics": relevance, reliability, and cost/benefit. The others are variations of these characteristics.

Concepts Statement 4, "Objectives of Financial Reporting by Nonbusiness Organizations," could be combined with CON 1. The only substantive differences between nonprofit organizations and business organizations are that nonprofits have contributed capital, which businesses do not, and business organizations have transactions with owners, which nonprofits do not. In business accounting there is no conceptual difference between accounting in financial institutions and accounting in manufacturing and marketing companies. The differences described above are at least as important as the differences between businesses and nonprofit organizations.

CON 6, "Elements of Financial Statements," has 110 paragraphs on business enterprises and 43 paragraphs on nonbusiness organizations. As was noted above, there is no need for this separation. Moreover, the structure of CON 6 has led to the issuance of FAS 130, "Comprehensive Income," which unfortunately plays down the importance of net income. This discrepancy is analyzed in Chapter 4.

Controversial Concepts

Most accounting issues are resolved by reference to generally accepted concepts. A few concepts are inadequate or no longer provide correct guidance for standards. They are discussed below.

Fair Value

"Fair value" refers to the amount an entity can expect to receive if it sells an item on the date of the financial statement.

CON 5, "Recognition and Measurement in Financial Statements of Business Enterprises," describes five types of measurement. Actually, experience shows that the only two measurement bases are historical cost and fair value. The others are minor variations.

In many cases the amount of a transaction could be measured by the agreement between two unrelated parties. A sale amount is the amount agreed to by a buyer and a seller. The acquisition of an asset is the amount agreed to by a purchaser and the entity that provides the goods or services. The accounting entry of this transaction is the agreed-upon amount. In 1992 the concept of fair value was introduced. Instead of being based on original cost, the amount was adjusted to the fair value of an asset at the end of the accounting period.

Currently, most transactions other than those involving

fixed assets are recorded at their fair value. Most liabilities are reported at their fair value because reliable estimates of their present value can be made.

The concept of fair value has an inherent problem. Because the fair value reported is as of the balance sheet date, that amount may be changed the next day. Users are, of course, interested in the fair value as of the date when they are examining the numbers. The reported fair value therefore may be obsolete. The reported amount cannot be the fair value as of the date when the reader examines the report. There is no way to determine what that amount is.

This concept is controversial. The buyer and the seller must agree on the amount of a purchase; the exchange price is in most cases the item's "fair value." If one of the parties is incompetent or is dominated by the other party, this generalization is not valid because one party has much more influence on the price than the other does. Recent transactions, especially those involving new enterprises or established enterprises that are going public, have fair values for their stock, which may soon turn out to be unrealistic. This situation is being studied carefully by the FASB and probably will lead to a circumscribed definition of fair value.

The fact that fixed assets transactions remain cost-based means that the balance sheet contains two types of items: fair value and cost. Therefore, the sum of asset amounts is not a meaningful number. This problem is discussed in Chapter 3.

For items other than fixed assets, the fair value is not tied to the acquisition cost. The problem here is that a reliable number for the fair value is not available. Various formulas for arriving at the fair value have been suggested, but all of them require an estimate of what the value of the asset will be in the future period in which the products, or a component of products, are sold. Often there is no way to make a reliable estimate. A major example of this problem is the treatment of stock options. The drafters of the Sarbanes-Oxley Act of 2002 were unable to agree on a solution, and so this issue was omitted from the law.

Derivatives

Investment transactions are becoming increasingly complicated. They are intended to take account of the relative risk
and reward in the instrument; hedging instruments are an example. There is no clear method of arriving at the fair value of
these transactions.

Consolidations

Accounting for the acquisition of one institution by a corporation is another example of this issue. The current treatment of
special purpose entities (SPEs) partnerships is an example
highlighted by the Enron Corporation.

Topics Not Discussed

In this book I do not discuss three topics that are related to
but are not a part of generally accepted accounting principles:
unethical behavior, auditing rules, and principle-based accounting.

Unethical Behavior

The Sarbanes-Oxley Act of 2002 placed much emphasis on the
ethics of those who prepare financial statements. The law,
medicine, engineering, auditing, and other professions have
rules about ethical behavior. State bodies that license professions have codes of ethics. Those bodies can disciple violators,
including canceling their licenses to engage in the profession.
Unfortunately, there is no professional regulating body for
managers. The Sarbanes-Oxley Act of 2002 requires that companies furnish a statement of their code of ethics if they have
one. Title 18 created a 25-year felony sentence for defrauding

shareholders of publicly traded companies. Chapter 63, Title 18, section 1348, adds a provision which would criminalize actions that defraud persons in connection with the securities of publicly traded companies or fraudulently obtain their money or property. The Public Oversight Board of the Securities and Exchange Commission (SEC) is considering rules for implementing the Sarbanes-Oxley Act of 2002 in regard to the responsibility of lawyers and auditors to act on their opinion that fraud has been committed.

If professionals steal money, lie, produce an inferior product, or commit other sins, their conduct is illegal and they can be punished in the courts. Some conduct is legal but unethical as defined in the code of professional conduct. These violations are much more difficult to identify and punish than are legal violations. For example, in *U.S. v. Simon* the U.S. Circuit Court of Appeals found a firm's auditors guilty of fraud even though their actions were legal.

An example of unethical behavior is excess compensation. Executives may take excessive compensation from the company, and this is unethical. However, defining what compensation is excessive is difficult. Despite the extensive criticism of excess compensation in certain companies, I know of no code of professional conduct that defines excess compensation in a measurable way.

Pundits in print and on television and members of congressional committees complain about the huge compensation paid to chief executive officers and other senior officials. They claim that certain officials' behavior is unethical even though it may be legal. The *Financial Times* calculated that the executives at the 25 largest American companies that went bankrupt in the last few years received $3.3 billion collectively in "share sales, payoffs, and other rewards." That huge amount is clearly unethical.

Ethical standards have been violated if the amount of compensation is judged to be unethical. However, Bill Gates has reported huge compensation from Microsoft, and no one has said that his compensation was unethical. Unless the critics can define "unethical compensation," their criticism is not helpful.

Even when the American Institute of Certified Public Accountants (AICPA) determined that accountants sanctioned by the SEC had committed violations, it closed the vast majority of those ethics cases without disciplinary action or public disclosure.

The prevalence of unethical behavior is indicated by the malpractice claims submitted to Continental Casualty Company, underwriters of the AICPA professional liability insurance program. Only 5 percent of the 22,000 claims insured by certified public accountant (CPA) firms engaged in revenue manipulation fraud. In 2002 the State of New Hampshire successfully sued Tyco International Corporation for $5 million for committing "misused corporate funds, made transactions without proper corporate approval and filed false and incomplete regulatory statements with the state."

I am convinced that the compensation of senior executives in some companies is too high, but I can't prove it, nor can I suggest a remedy. Therefore, I do not attempt to do that in this book.

Auditing Rules

Acceptable financial statements must be prepared in accordance with generally accepted accounting principles (GAAP). Compliance usually is determined by CPAs who are contracted by the reporting entity for this purpose. If the financial statements do not conform to GAAP in all material respects, the CPA so states. If such a statement is made about a business organization, the SEC immediately will prohibit trading with that organization on a stock exchange. Most users will not accept such a qualified statement. As a practical matter, therefore, the only statements issued are those consistent with GAAP; that is, the draft statements are revised until an unqualified opinion is given by the auditor. In arriving at their conclusion, the auditors must exercise "due diligence." That is, they must do enough work to be satisfied with their conclusion that the financial statements report what they are supposed to report.

The SEC also may challenge an item in an entity's financial statements. Those challenges may lead to a change in the financial statements.[4]

If there is disagreement about an accounting rule, the auditor's opinion governs. If management and the auditor cannot resolve a difference of opinion, either management accepts the opinion or the auditor resigns. When the entity is multinational, a decision not to accept the auditor's opinion is extremely rare. The auditor will resign in that case, but there are only a few accounting firms that have offices throughout the world, and those firms are the only alternatives. For small firms that operate primarily within the United States, this problem does not arise: A company may select any of dozens of American firms.

Some entities change auditors every few years to reduce the bias that may creep in because of familiarity. The Sarbanes-Oxley Act of 2002 requires that auditors be changed every five years.

Changes also have been made in the AICPA's auditing standards. However, those changes are separate from the standards of financial accounting and therefore are not discussed in this book.

Principle-Based Accounting

Some pundits and legislatures have recommended that the current set of accounting standards be scrapped and replaced by a set of "principles." I do not know what they mean by this.

A principle-based approach would be similar to scrapping all the rules about vehicle traffic, one of which is that drivers should not exceed a reasonable speed. It would scrap the rules for left turns, red lights, yellow lights, green lights, yielding to pedestrians, using directional signals, stopping at railroad crossings, passing another car, using high and low headlight beams, following a fire truck, multilane highways, hills, curves, residential areas, encountering a work site, intersections, schools, stopping for a school bus, commuter lanes, not tailgating, driving after consuming too much alcohol or drugs, driving in snow or rain, child restraints, and emergency vehicles. Law officers, would have the impossible task of interpreting this principle, and lawyers would have a great opportunity to interpret it in specific situations. It eventually would result in a set of common laws comparable to the present rules.

A principle of financial accounting is that revenue is recognized in the period in which goods and services are delivered and in the amount received or expected to be received. Companies may have different opinions about the recognition of leases with various qualifications. They may differ about purchases that will be paid for with various time qualifications. Real estate developers differ about the timing of revenues and costs for various stages of a project. They differ with payments on borrowed funds or equities. They differ with the timing of revenue recognition of companies with oil or other mineral deposits. Companies differ in regard to revenues from research or partially developed research projects. Construction companies may differ about the timing of revenue recognition in various stages of a project. Motion picture producers may not know the revenue for a film until well after the year has ended. Similarly, software producers whose revenue is derived from license agreements may not know the revenue until after the period has ended.

The FASB is considering responses to its exposure draft "Proposal for a Principles-Based Approach to U.S. Standards Setting," which was expected on January 3, 2003. This document is intended to list general principles that are more specific than the existing concepts statements but less specific than financial accounting standards. It contains an illustration of a possible principle for the current Statement 133. Statement 133 has 163 pages of small type; it surely needs condensing.

The other illustration relates to a revision of Statement 34, which deals with the recognition of equity interest as a cost. The proposal does not shorten the existing text; instead, it suggests additions that deal with specific topics related to equity interest. Those additions should have been made in Statement 34 and are discussed at length in Chapter 4.

The same general approach can be used for other paragraphs while maintaining the specifics that are needed. Furthermore, the standards in general can be cut at least in half by eliminating unnecessary background and other material; this is discussed in more detail in Chapter 9.

In his testimony of February 14, 2002, Robert K. Herdman, chief accountant of the SEC, suggested a compromise solution that would use general principles whenever possible and supply more detail when it was necessary to be specific.

Measurement Concepts in Financial Accounting

Double Entry

For more than 500 years accounting has been a dual-aspect system. Each transaction reports one or more debit amounts and one or more credit amounts, and the sum of the debits must equal the sum of the credits. This practice helps accountants analyze transactions properly and detect certain types of errors. In a current balance sheet this requirement is expressed by the equation Total Assets = Total Liabilities + Total Equity. This is why a balance sheet may contain an asset or liability item that is equal to the credit or debit adjustment that converts accounting income to taxable income. The equity item is necessary to maintain the equality of the balance sheet even though it does not measure the true "equity" of the company. This is the case because the asset amount does not measure the actual assets of the company.

There is no requirement that this equality be reported, however. The auditor determines whether the equality exists. If it does not, the auditor will say so, but this occurs only rarely.

Usefulness

The numbers reported in the measurement system should be useful to the intended readers. In financial accounting the readers are assumed to be creditors, investors, and other outside parties who want information about individual entities. Presumably, those users have a general knowledge of accounting.

The balance sheet for the federal government is not useful. It is impossible to report all the assets of the federal government. Therefore, the balance sheet cannot meet the criteria of usefulness. I don't know anyone who would use a federal government balance sheet. I discuss federal accounting in Chapter 10.

The balance sheet and income statement of certain government agencies and information about categories of assets within an agency may be useful. Although it is not feasible to list the cost of all assets in the U.S. Department of Defense (DoD), for example, records of certain individual defense assets, such as inventory, are useful to DoD management.

Informed Users

Users of accounting information are assumed to understand the nature of the applicable rules and the entities to which they apply; they are "informed." Novices may not know about or understand those rules. This disadvantage can be overcome partially because of the availability of texts, lectures, and articles on accounting. Those who make the rules are not required to explain them.

Of course, there is disagreement about how much users are assumed to know. For example, in the construction and housing industries there are at least three ways to measure the square footage of a building: (1) the total space within the exterior walls, (2) the total space less the space used for equipment and corridors, and (3) the space usable by renters. Members of those industries understand what square footage means in a given context, and so they do not need explanations. People outside the industries may be misled unless the relevant definition is explained. Similarly, members of the sea transportation industry know that a measurement ton is a measure of volume: 30 cubic feet. In most other situations a ton is a measure of weight.

Entity

Financial accounting reports the performance and status of an entity. In general, an entity is a body owned and/or controlled by an identifiable person, partners, shareholders, or another governing body. There are differences of opinion about what constitutes an accounting entity. An entity may consist of a number of subordinate entities. The financial statements produced for those entities are "consolidated" financial statements.

Required Statements

The accounting system has two essential required financial statements for entities: a statement that reports the flows during an accounting period and a statement that reports the status of the entity at the period's end. Two additional statements are required: a statement of cash flows (discussed in Chapter 5) and a statement of changes in equity (discussed in Chapter 6). Those two statements contain information derived from the statement on status and the statement on flows.

    The amounts reported in those statements must conform to

rules established by the FASB. They are called "standards." The standards are derived from "concepts." Concepts are general statements, and standards are the application of those statements to specific situations. There are only six financial accounting concepts totaling 158 pages but over 2,000 pages of standards. Accountants must comply with the standards, but they need not know about the concepts, although this knowledge may be helpful background information. In addition to the standards, corporations are required by the SEC to report a section called "Management Discussion and Analysis (MD&A)."

Except for the future estimates mentioned above, the amounts reported on financial statements are not influenced by personal opinions, including those of management. They are "objective," which means that they include the numbers in an actual transaction, numbers that are approximately the same as the transaction numbers, and fair value for financial items whenever that is attainable. Management's opinion of the entity's status may be stated in the MD&A section of the financial statements, but it should not appear in the financial statements themselves. Like most estimates made by persons whose performance is being reported on, these opinions are likely to be biased.

The Sarbanes-Oxley Act of 2002 has many references to the MD&A section but none to the financial statements themselves. Subsequent to the passage of the law, the SEC established specific requirements for the material to be reported in the MD&A section. Those requirements applied to corporations with revenue of more than $2 billion.

Required Supplemental Information

In addition to the information described above, entities are required to report certain information in the notes section of the financial statement. For example, entities that operate in more than one industry are required to report flow information about each major industry segment.

Information is either flow information or status information. The definition of a term that measures flows may affect the way that term is treated in the status report. If depreciation expense in the income statement is derived from an asset's cost, for instance, the balance sheet number for that asset also must be based on cost. The definition of one of those terms has to be accepted as governing. Currently, despite some comments to the contrary in FASB documents, rules for terms in the income statement are more important than rules for the balance sheet.

The flow statement's bottom line, "net income," is more important and is used more frequently than are the "total assets," "total liabilities," or "total equity" listed on the balance sheet.[5] This is significant because for some issues a choice must be made between a standard that arrives at a useful measure of net income and a standard that arrives at useful balance sheet amounts. In last-in, first-out (LIFO) inventory, for example, the balance sheet amounts are not of much use. The concept should state that when a choice must be made, a good measure of income takes precedence over a good balance sheet. Some balance sheet items result from the measurement rules for revenues or expenses. As an example, the amount of deferred income taxes is derived from the revenue item on the income statement. In fact, there is no observable asset called "deferred income taxes."

Extraordinary Items

A balance sheet may contain "extraordinary items." These are unusual, nonrecurring items that are identified separately from nonordinary items. There is no standard that defines the term more specifically.

Financial accounting uses but does not define the term "extraordinary."

Historical

Financial statements are literally historical; the amounts reported describe the entity's past financial status and flows.

The FASB requires the publication of quarterly interim statements, but the rules for those statements differ slightly from the rules governing the annual financial statements mentioned above.

Future Estimates

Some items in financial statements are necessarily based on estimates of what will happen in the future. These cases usually are obvious. The gross amount of accounts receivable is reduced by estimated future bad debts. Depreciation expense requires an estimate of the future life of the asset.

Investment analysts use the financial information, plus other information, to estimate an entity's real status, but those estimates are not reported in financial statements and should not be. Financial statements are strictly reports of what has happened and what the current status is. Analysts use this and other information to estimate what the status will be in the future.

Monetary Items

Financial statements include only items whose magnitude can be stated in monetary amounts. Therefore, they exclude many important items that are necessary to understand an entity's performance and status. They do not include the entity's reputation with consumers, the ability of the chief executive officer, new products that are likely to be valuable when they are introduced, or the skills and morale of employees. Words and qualitative attributes obviously cannot be added to num-

bers, but they are appropriately included in the MD&A section of an annual report.

Matching

The expenses of a year are items (1) associated with the products delivered and (2) other costs incurred or recognized in
that year. The focus here is on products. As was mentioned
above, if an item is reported at fair value, the resulting gain or
loss in a period is recognized.

Currently, there is much criticism of financial statements
that do not report the value of new products even though the
probable future profit of those products may be huge. One example is a drug recently approved by the U.S. Food and Drug
Administration that probably will benefit millions of people.
Its value is subjective information, which might be reported
in the MD&A section. These items are not reported at their estimated present value. This explains why the stock market
value of some companies differs drastically from the amount
reported in their financial statements.

Conservatism

The amounts reported for certain terms are conservative. This
means that revenues are increases in equity that are recognized when they are reasonably certain but are decreased as
soon as they are reasonably possible. The treatment of expenses is therefore more conservative than the treatment of
revenues. There is disagreement about the precise meaning of
this term.

Time Period

Although some people maintain that accounting information
eventually may be available for reporting as soon as an event

occurs, I think this is unrealistic. Financial statements are published annually, and certain reports are published quarterly. Because many items are reported at fair value, which can change daily, more frequent information is unrealistic.

Materiality

Trivial matters are disregarded, but all-important matters are disclosed. There are differences of opinion about what is important or material. The general rule is that a number is material if it could affect a user's judgment about an entity.

Private Information

Some important information may be as useful to a competitor as it is to an investor. That information therefore should not be in the public financial statements.

Going Concern Concept

Financial statements assume that an entity is not going to be liquidated for at least one year after the end of the accounting period. If the entity is likely to be liquidated, the solvency laws require that special standards apply to its financial statements.

Notes

[1] The Financial Accounting Standards Board does not agree with my list. See the comment by David Mosso in FASB *Viewpoints,* September 30, 1998, 5–6.

[2] Matthew Bovee, Michael Ettredge, Rajendra P. Srivastava, and Milos Vasarhelyi, "Assessing the 7/31/2000 XBRL Taxonomy for Digital Financial Reports of Commercial and Industrial Firms," July 20, 2001. XBRL website.

[3] For example, the FASB uses "not-for-profit," but the dictionary, the Internal Revenue Service, and other sources use "nonprofit."

[4] Noncompliance seems to have become more common in recent years. The

SEC required a restatement of 49 financial statements a year, and there were 91 restatements in 1998, 150 in 1999, and 156 in 2000. FEI Research Foundation, *Quantitative Measures of the Quality of Financial Reporting*, June 7, 2001. Many of these increases are the inevitable result of increased complexity in the transactions.

[5] Paragraph 43 of Concepts Statement No. 1 (CON 1) states, "The primary focus of financial reporting is information about an enterprise's performance provided by measures of earning and its components."

3
THE FINANCIAL POSITION STATEMENT

The balance sheet, which also is known as the statement of financial position, has very limited usefulness in its current format because it does not report an entity's financial position. Uninformed people assume that the balance sheet measures financial status; its failure to do that gives accounting a bad name.

Although a financial statement called a "balance sheet" was used for 500 years, its content was not similar to that of a modern balance sheet until well into the twentieth century. In the twenty-first century a balance sheet has very limited value. It reports some assets at fair value and other assets at an amount based on cost because their fair value cannot be measured. A basic rule of arithmetic states that the addition of numbers derived from different measurement systems produces a meaningless total.

In its current form a balance sheet does not report an entity's financial position. The asset side does not, and cannot, report all the resources that an entity owns or controls. Moreover, some assets are not reported because neither their fair value nor their cost can be measured. Examples include the value of brands, loyal customers, new products, and the quality of management.

With the increasing importance of those intangibles, especially knowledge-based assets, the balance sheet has become even less meaningful as a report of an entity's "real" assets. Because equity is the difference between assets and liabilities, the amount reported as owners' equity is not meaningful.

Many articles in economics journals assume that the balance sheet does report fair values.

I suggest replacing this misleading financial statement with a new statement that measures solvency. Solvency shows important information that is not currently reported in any required financial statement. A statement of solvency would not report fixed assets because those numbers are based on cost. In a solvency statement all the numbers are derived from a single measurement system; it is based on fair value. Preparing this statement would require only one new accounting rule: a standard that describes the elements of a report on solvency.

This new statement would measure an entity's ability to meet its obligations when they come due. This is a well-established concept in both law and auditing and would provide a practical report of an important aspect of an entity's financial position.

A conventional balance sheet may continue to be needed for public utilities and other organizations whose selling prices are the sum of the historical costs of fixed assets and a profit margin.

Background

The basis of modern accounting is the dual-aspect concept used in Italy in the early fifteenth century and stated in the text of Luca Pacioli's *Summa* (1494). Pacioli stated that accounting should measure two equal aspects of every transaction. He labeled one aspect "debit" and the other "credit." That distinction led to a balance sheet with two sides. The left side reported assets, and the right side reported claims against those assets. The asset amount was cash plus accounts receivable as those terms are used today. The totals of the two sides were equal; they balanced. That idea persists today.

Pacioli's system reported only cash transactions. It was widely used by companies that sent a ship or fleet of ships to explore foreign territories. At the end of the voyage a balance sheet was prepared. Assets on the left side represented the monetary value of the goods that were brought back. Claims on the right side reported how those amounts were to be divided among the crew members and the investors who financed the voyage.

The right side was divided into two parts. One part, called "liabilities," reported the claims of outside parties; the other part, called "equity," reported the owners' interest. The resulting equation is still used today: Assets = Liabilities + Equity.

Accrual Accounting

Until the nineteenth century balance sheets continued to report only cash transactions, although records of receivables and payables were maintained earlier. In the 1800s aspects of accrual accounting were introduced, but they were used by only a few corporations until the middle of that century.

Accrual accounting reports were prepared for management's use and for investors and creditors. Because few corporations obtained funds from lenders or investors other than in the form of short-term loans, there were only a few of those reports until the middle of the nineteenth century.

Accrual accounting measures the financial performance of an entity in an accounting period as the difference between its revenues and its expenses. Revenues are resources *earned* during the relevant period, and expenses are resources *used* during that period. Accrual accounting is used principally to measure income, which is reported in a flow report, that is, a report of the flow of revenues and expenses during an accounting period. The other commonly used financial statement is a status report, that is, a report of the entity's financial status at the end of the accounting period.

There are two types of status reports. One type reports as assets all the financial and nonfinancial resources owned by the entity, and it reports owners' equity. The other type reports only financial assets and therefore cannot report owners' equity. This type of report is called a balance sheet, although, unlike the "usual" balance sheet, it does not report long-lived nonfinancial assets such as land, plant, and equipment. A more accurate title would be a solvency statement because a solvency statement does not report long-lived nonfinancial assets.

In the nineteenth century the literature did not distinguish between these two types of status reports. *A History of Accountancy in the United States* by Previts and Merino (1998) describes many status reports, most of which clearly are solvency statements. Balance sheets containing fixed assets were reported primarily by public utilities and other regulated industries.

Railroads were the first corporations in the United States to prepare accrual financial statements. They were the first entities to require outside financing and the first to be regulated. They provided elaborate financial statements to investors and regulators, some of which were as many as 50 pages long. By the mid-nineteenth century those statements included charges for depreciation or its equivalent (such as "annual decay"). The focus was on the income statement. Assets were reported, but not on a separate report called a balance sheet (Brockholdt, 1978).

The statement that balance sheets have been widely used for 500 years is too broad, therefore. They were used for ventures throughout that period and for regulated industries beginning in the nineteenth century and that is all.

The Sixteenth Amendment

The passage of the Sixteenth Amendment to the U.S. Constitution in 1913 and the income tax statute of that year led to the widespread use of accrual accounting because depreciation and other noncash expenses were tax-deductible items. Balance sheets began to report receivables and payables, and income statements reported both cash and noncash revenues and expenses. Accounting for income taxes also led to the use of the balance sheet asset "deferred income taxes." This was necessary to have debits equal credits even though this item was not actually a definable asset. Most, but not all, items were reported at historical cost. The principal exception was inventory, which was reported at market value if market value was lower than cost, in accordance with the concept of conservatism.

Early Twentieth Century

In the United States upward revaluations of assets were popular before the 1929 stock market crash. What was written up before the crash had to be written down afterward. The idea that "false" financial statements were an important cause of the crash seems to be the reason that the Securities and Exchange Commission (SEC) required the use of historical cost. (Actually, most later write-downs related to intangibles rather than to tangible fixed assets.) Solvency was measured by the ratio of current assets to current liabilities.

Realization Concept

Until recently standards-setting bodies accepted the realization concept. This concept prohibits writing up the value of assets even if their value as of the balance sheet date exceeds their cost because the increase in value has not been realized.[1]

The 1965 Concepts and Standards Committee of the American Accounting Association took the same view. It concluded, "The accounting entity should be a party to the market transaction before realized revenue is recognized." The committee did predict the change that was to come, however:

> The winds of change are blowing hard in the accounting profession, and it is only a matter of time before they ruffle the calm of realization in published financial statements and in the accounting profession.[2]

In July 2002 the SEC questioned Merck & Co about its treatment of copayments. Copayments are payments consumers make to pharmacies to buy prescription drugs under health insurance plans. They ordinarily are made to the retail pharmacy, not to Merck directly. Under certain circumstances Merck would be liable, but it ordinarily is not involved. Merck credited $12 billion in revenue over the previous three years, stating that those payments were in accordance with generally accepted accounting principles (GAAP). Some accountants concurred; others did not.

Experiment with Replacement Cost

Beginning in 1978, the Financial Accounting Standards Board (FASB) experimented with reporting fixed assets at replacement cost rather than historical cost. That requirement was stated in the following Financial Accounting Standards (FAS's): 33 (1979); 39, 40, and 41 (1980); 46 (1981); 54, 69, and 70 (1982); and 82 (1984). Large corporations were required to prepare balance sheets and income statements on this basis. FAS89 (1986) abandoned the experiment by changing the rule from a requirement to a suggestion. This was the last that was heard of accounting for replacement costs.

In the 1940s and 1950s there were many articles in the literature concerning whether accounting should measure the maintenance of financial capital or physical capital. Nothing came of that discussion. In fact, accounting cannot measure either goal except in an economy in which new assets are the same as the assets they replace, and that rarely happens.

Shift to Fair Value

The corporate failures of the 1960s and 1970s demonstrated that neither net income on the income statement nor working capital on the balance sheet could adequately explain the cause of financial difficulties. Solvency, as measured by the difference between all financial assets and liabilities, was not identified explicitly on those statements (Heath, 1978). Solvency would measure that difference. A report of changes in solvency measures the difference between amounts at one period and amounts for the preceding period.

As was described in Chapter 2, beginning in 1982, the FASB required that certain financial assets be reported at their fair value (i.e., market value) as of the balance sheet date. This was first stated in FAS60, "Accounting and Reporting by Insurance Enterprises." From that year on many standards contained requirements for reporting fair value: FAS105 (1990), 107 (1991), 113 (1992), 115 (1993), 118 and 119 (1994), 125 (1996), 129 (1997), 133 and 134 (1998), 137 (1999), and 138 and 139 (2000).

As of 2002 the FASB began a continuing study of financial instruments in which its goal was to account for all financial instruments at their fair value.

Although the FASB pronouncements focused on the fair value of assets, most liabilities already are reported at fair value even though that term is not used.

The FASB issued CON 7, "Using Cash Flow Information and Present Value in Accounting Measurement," in 1999, its first new concepts statement in 15 years. It gave strong support to the concept of fair value.

Many texts and articles by economists during that period implicitly assumed that financial statements reported assets' fair value or the accountant's best estimate of fair value. Students learned that misconception from economics courses.

This is why the accounting and economics departments do not get along well in some schools.

Strangely, the FASB has said very little over the years about solvency. The term is mentioned in CON 1, 2, 4, and 5 in sentences that list uses for balance sheets, but solvency is neither defined nor used in any FASB statement.[3] The Joint Working Group of Standards issued a report on December 22, 2000, that proposed reporting almost all financial instruments at fair value on the balance sheet and reporting changes in fair value on the income statement.[4]

In summary, for centuries a status report of cash receipts and disbursements was an important financial statement. There is a better system. It was called a balance sheet, but it did not contain all the items that are in a modern balance sheet. In the nineteenth century status reports were expanded to include accruals, but assets still were measured at cost, with no deduction for depreciation. The income statement became more important than the balance sheet even though the FASB did not explicitly recognize that fact. About 10 years ago the balance sheet began to report fair values for some, but not all, assets. Consequently, total assets and equity became meaningless numbers because items were reported in accordance with two different measurement systems.

Recognition of Solvency in Other Countries

In the United Kingdom early legislation required companies to report on solvency, with an additional requirement that capital be maintained before dividends were paid. There was no prohibition of asset revaluations, but case law encouraged a conservative attitude on the part of auditors. If there was any doubt about the solvency of a dividend-paying company, auditors were to ensure that assets were not stated above selling prices. Historical cost could be higher than selling price, but after an 1889 case (*Lee v. Neuchatel Asphalte Co.*) the view was that if a dividend-paying company later collapsed, the auditors were less likely to be held liable if they had accepted assets *at* historical cost and more likely to be sued if they stated assets *above* historical cost (Edey and Panitpakdi, 1956). This conservative approach remained in force until the 1948 Companies Act was passed (Edwards, 1989).

That legislation was used as the basis for similar legislation in Australia and New Zealand. Those laws contained an over-riding requirement that a balance sheet give a "true and fair" view of an entity's financial position. That requirement led to the conclusion that historical cost might not meet this stan-dard and that some other valuation was called for (Beckett, 1966). After 1948 asset revaluations, especially of land and buildings, became increasingly popular (Whittington, 1971). However, the revalued assets were not necessarily stated at either fair value or market value.

Current British regulations accommodate valuations, with the ability to choose upper-limit valuations that are based on estimated future cash flows with no discounting require-ments.

Defects of the Balance Sheet

A balance sheet has two weaknesses: It combines unlike num-bers, and it omits some of an entity's assets.

Assets on a balance sheet are measured in two fundamen-tally different ways. *Monetary* assets such as cash, cash equiv-alents, equity securities, and loans are measured at their fair value as of the balance sheet date. Other assets, including plant, equipment, research in progress, goodwill, and similar purchased intangibles, are reported variously at cost, at the fraction of acquisition cost that has not yet been counted as expenses, or at fair value if it is lower than cost, as in the case of inventory.

A basic rule of arithmetic is that unlike items cannot be summed; one cannot add apples and oranges. To illustrate, imagine a highway weigh station that weighs trucks and their contents to ensure compliance with highway weight limita-tions. If the trucks were measured in pounds and the contents in kilograms, the sum of their weights would be neither pounds nor kilograms. To produce a meaningful sum, the weight of the truck body must be converted to kilograms or the weight of the contents must be converted to pounds. The fair value of most nonfinancial items cannot be measured. Because some asset items are reported at fair value and other items are reported at cost (or a number based on cost), the total obtained by adding those numbers is meaningless.

For example, consider two companies with the following reported assets:

	A	B
Marketable securities (at fair value)	$500,000	$400,000
Plant and equipment (at depreciated cost)	400,000	500,000
Total assets	$900,000	$900,000

The two $900,000 totals are meaningless. They do not mean that A and B have the same amount of assets, that A has more assets than B, or that B has more assets than A.

Moreover, the balance sheet does not report many valuable assets, among them trademarks, owned channels of distribution, brands, loyal customers, and patents, unless those assets were purchased. The value of certain computer software programs that have been created is not reported even though these products are judged by investors to be worth millions or even billions of dollars.

Accounting reports bricks-and-mortar assets in great detail, but it treats human resources only as expenses, not as assets. Even though the real value of a research laboratory lies in the skill of the researchers and the way in which they are organized, accounting measures only the laboratory facilities and equipment as assets.

Some assets are recorded at what the FASB calls the "cost accrual method." In effect, they are reported on the balance sheet at an amount that offsets an income statement item. As was noted above, deferred tax assets and liabilities are reported at the amounts deferred rather than at the fair value of those amounts.

Most liabilities—amounts owed to employees, accounts payable, income tax owed, bond indebtedness—are measured at the present value of the amount that actually is owed. For bonds issued at par, par is the present value of the interest payments plus the present value of the repayment of principal. If the bonds are not issued at par, amortization of the discount or premium brings the number to present value.

Because the asset side of the balance sheet does not report a meaningful total, the number for equity, which is the difference between assets and liabilities, is also meaningless because it does not report what the shareholder interest is worth. "Net worth" is a misnomer. Analysts pay little attention to this number except in analyzing entities, such as mutual funds, whose assets are almost entirely monetary.

For these reasons, the balance sheet is literally a "sheet of balances" (as it was designated by FASB member Bob Sprouse). Individual items are useful, but the totals do not mean anything. Informed users know this and pay little attention to those totals. They disregard the nonmonetary amounts and use the monetary amounts as a guide in measuring solvency.

The Solvency Statement

Although solvency is a rare topic in accounting literature, it has been a topic in common law and legislation for many years.

There are two ways to measure an entity's financial viability: liquidity and solvency. The two terms are in fact different despite implications by some authors that they have the same meaning.

Liquidity is an entity's ability to meet its current obligations. It is measured by the current ratio and the acid-test ratio. The current ratio is the ratio of current assets to current liabilities. As a rough rule of thumb, a ratio of 2 to 1 indicates that a company is satisfactorily liquid. The acid-test ratio, or quick ratio, excludes inventory and intangible assets from the calculation. It requires a ratio of better than 1 to 1. Both measures are easily calculated from data on the balance sheet.

An entity is solvent if the fair value of its assets at least equals the claims against the entity as measured by its liabilities. Solvency is not reported on the balance sheet, but it can be calculated from the financial items that are reported.

I suggest that the balance sheet be converted to a report that measures solvency. Exhibit 1 shows a sample solvency statement.

Like a balance sheet, a solvency statement is historical. It reports the situation as of the end of the period, a date that will have passed by the time the report is issued. Unlike a balance sheet, the fair value of each asset and liability item reported on a solvency statement is known or can be estimated with reasonable accuracy; nevertheless, the basis for each estimate should be shown so that the reader may make his or her own judgment about the value.

Many of the items on a statement of affairs are similar to the items on a solvency statement. A solvency statement is similar to the statement of affairs that is prepared when an entity is about to be liquidated. The measurement concepts are the same; the principal difference is that the solvency statement is prepared as of the end of the accounting period, with no evidence that the entity is about to be declared bankrupt or otherwise go out of business.

Although the numbers reported in the statement of affairs refer to their value as of a fairly recent date, the numbers for many assets require an estimate of the amount that will be realized when they are disposed of; the prospective buyer may estimate the present value of future earnings from them. Similarly, for liabilities, the amount is the present value of the amount that will be paid in the future, and the creditor will accept the present value of that amount or whatever amount the bankruptcy court determines.

A solvency statement cannot measure the current amount because the situation may have changed since the statement date. Nevertheless, a solvency statement is a useful starting

Exhibit 1. Waterman Company Solvency Statement

As of December 31, 2001 Dollars in Millions

Current Assets		Current Liabilities	
Cash and cash equivalents	$17	Accounts payable	$72
Marketable securities	97	Salary and wages	15
Accounts and notes	51	payable	
receivable (net)	51	Notes payable	14
Inventories	132	Debt current portion	78
Prepaid expenses	48	Other current liabilities	22
Other current assets	74		
Total current assets	$419	Total current liabilities	$201

Other Monetary Assets		Other Liabilities	
Noncurrent notes receivable	$92	Noncurrent debt	$652
Investment in debt securities	206	Pension and other	201
Bonds held to maturity	341	benefits	
Investment in equity	179	Noncurrent compen-	132
securities		sation	
Capital leases	464	Commitments	21
Real estate mortgages	26	Other liabilities	40
Deferred income taxes	23		
Preferred stock	42		
Total solvency assets	$1,792	Total liabilities	$1,247
		Net solvency	545
		Total liabilities and	$1,792
		net solvency	

Note: Prior-year numbers are omitted to save space.

point. In general, the assets used to measure solvency are the financial items whose fair value can be estimated reliably. These items include loans, bonds, stock, and other monetary assets except inventory owned by the entity.

The present values of the entity's financial obligations are the fair value of liabilities. These are the amounts that now are, or should be, reported.

My proposal retains two concepts that are inconsistent with the fair-value concept: the realization concept and the conversation concept. The current emphasis on fair values is consistent with these concepts.

The realization concept relates only to inventory and the cost of sales. For reasons given below, if fair value were used for these items, the effect on net income of departing from this concept would lead to an unrealistic measure of income.

The conservatism concept also relates primarily to inventory and the cost of sales. It is one of the reasons for reporting inventory at the lower of cost or market.

For other items, my proposal accepts these concepts.

Sources of Information on Solvency

Accounting literature in the United States says almost nothing about the solvency concept. No FASB standard deals with this topic. The American Institute of Certified Public Accountants (AICPA) *Statement on Auditing Standards* No. 59, "The Auditor's Consideration of an Entity's Ability to Continue as a Going Concern," has some generalizations that deal with what the auditor should consider but nothing about the relevant calculations.

In contrast with the paucity of information in accounting literature, much attention in regard to solvency is given to legislation, common law, and the legal literature. There are several legal definitions of solvency, but the differences among those definitions are small. *Black's Law Dictionary* has probably the generally accepted definition; its primary definition is "the ability to pay debts as they mature and come due." This is followed by several definitions taken from legislation and case law. Those definitions use similar words for the same idea.

Title 11 of the U.S. Code has a lengthy discussion of the definition of solvency and of broad principles for applying that definition in bankruptcy courts. The Uniform Fraudulent Transfer Act in some states and the Uniform Fraudulent Conveyance Act in other states describe the approach to measuring solvency in certain situations. The legislation does not discuss the details of how solvency should be measured, however.

In general, the law requires the use of fair value when those values exist and the use of appraised value in measuring other assets. Making a reliable appraisal at the end of each accounting period is obviously not feasible as a basis for an annual solvency statement.

The best source of principles for the measurement of solvency is case law. The most relevant cases are referred to in the legislation mentioned above.

International Accounting Standard 40, "Investment Property" (2000), has a discussion of balance sheet items that should be included.

Details of the Statement

Like the balance sheet, the solvency statement should report assets on the left-hand side and liabilities, which are claims against those assets, on the right-hand side.

The asset side should report all assets whose fair value as of the statement date can be measured reliably. These consist of current assets, financial instruments, and possibly some nonfinancial assets, as described below.

Current Assets. Current assets are assets that will be converted to cash in the near future. In most entities the "future" is one year. In entities whose operating cycle is longer than one year, such as distilleries whose inventory is aged for several years, "future" means the length of the normal production cycle. The amount reported on a solvency statement should be the same as the amount now reported on a balance sheet.

Gross amounts of receivables should be reduced by an allowance for bad debts, just as they are on a balance sheet. This allowance reduces the gross amount of receivables to its fair value.

The rules for inventory should be those currently used. Most inventory items are reported at cost. Precious metals and agricultural products with well-known market values are reported at fair value. There are sound reasons for these rules.

Inventory should be reported at cost or at market value if its market value is lower than cost. Inventory amounts should not be reported at either replacement cost or last-in, first-out (LIFO) cost.[5] The inventory amount should not be increased if market value exceeds cost; that would result in recognition of revenue before the goods are sold, which is inconsistent with the realization concept as it was explained above. Decreasing inventory if market value is lower than cost is required by the conservatism concept.

This treatment of inventory results in a collision between two concepts: the fair value concept and the realization concept. I believe that the current practice should be continued even though merchandise inventory would not be reported at fair value. If fair value exceeds cost, reporting inventory at its fair value would result in a peculiar income statement. The excess of fair value over cost would add to revenue, and the effect would be to increase the gross margin and net income. Both increases may give the wrong impression about sales. The current fair value as of the balance sheet date may be different from the actual sales price. If the sales price is lower than the fair value on the solvency statement, there will be an expense, and that would be a curious number.

I do not believe that sales revenue should be different from the amount that actually is realized when the goods are delivered, adjusted for an allowance for bad debts. If the fair-value concept were applied, an adjustment to the solvency statement amount would be necessary in many cases, and it would generate more confusion than useful information.

As was noted earlier, although assets are reported at their historical amount as of the date of the financial statement, this amount necessarily includes estimates of future performance or certain types of assets.

Financial Instruments.   Financial instruments are bonds, stocks, loans, and capital leases owned by an entity. Many of these items have quoted market values and should be reported at those amounts. Items for which no reasonable estimate of fair value can be made should be excluded. The FASB is considering the treatment of instruments that are hedges or derivatives and other aspects of financial assets.

The FASB may decide that measuring fair value leads to undesirable volatility. If that occurs, volatility can be reduced by means of a rule that requires using an average of the last seven days' amounts.

Certain Nonfinancial Assets.   Some nonfinancial assets have characteristics similar to those of the financial assets that are reported at fair value. Their fair value can be measured reliably, and that value may exceed the costs incurred in acquiring them. For financial assets, the gain of the difference between cost and fair value would be reported as an addition to net income in the current period. These assets differ from financial assets in that they are products, and revenues from the sale of products are reported in the period in which the products were delivered or in the period in which the revenue on interest-bearing assets was earned. Recognizing fair value for these items in the current period would violate the realization concept, which states that revenue should be recognized only when products are delivered or when interest and rental revenues are earned. With the increased emphasis on fair value, some of these assets should be considered for inclusion in the solvency statement. I do not mean to imply that they should be treated in that way; that would represent a drastic change in financial accounting. Reporting revenue in one period with an implicit agreement that the products will be returned in the following period should not be recognized as a method for reporting revenue.

The solvency statement does not cause these problems; they are the consequence of extending the fair-value idea to an increasing number of items. Reporting all those items at fair value is highly unlikely. The central problem is where to draw the line. Consider the following examples.

Capital Leases

Capital leases are leases for essentially the expected life of an asset. FAS13 requires that the present value of the stream of lease payments be reported as a gross amount on the lessor's balance sheet, but that amount is reduced by the amount of "unearned income" implicit in the lease agreement. The unearned income account is reduced, and revenue is recognized in each accounting period. Consequently, no profit is reported for the year in which the lease agreement becomes effective except the interest revenue earned in that year. Should the fair value be reported as an asset on the solvency statement? Yes, provided that the basis for the "fair value" is explained.

Other Leases

The owner of an office building, a warehouse, or an apartment building may lease the property for a long period but for less than its expected life. In most cases, lease payments are stated in the contract; in others, the payments are adjusted for changes in an index of inflation. Should the present value of the payments, including an estimate of the inflation component, be reported as an asset?

In a study by Nailor and Lennard,[6] the authors note that

"alternatively, a minority of participants in the G4+1 second study believes that the asset that results from entering into a lease contract is the leased property itself. Under this approach, liabilities arising from lease contracts include not only the obligation to pay rent over the lease term, but also the obligation to return the leased property to the lessor at the end of the lease term unless the lease is renewed or extended.

"A majority of the participants in the second study concluded that each separate right arising out of a lease contract represents an asset and each separate obligation represents a liability that lessees need to recognize and account for individually. Under this approach, at the commencement of a lease, lessees record an asset and liability equal to the present value of the committed rental payments *and* an asset and a liability equal to the fair value of any renewal option, residual value guarantee and/or contingent rent provisions in the lease. Where fair values are not readily observable, they must be estimated."

I believe that accounting for leases should be reexamined by the FASB. I do not discuss this topic further here.

Timber

Timber and other forest products increase in value each year. FAS 40 required in effect that the fair value be reported, although the term "fair value" was not used. FAS 40 was rescinded in 1986 by FAS 89. Should reporting fair value be reinstated?

Oil, Gas, and Other Minerals

There has been much discussion about the amount to be reported as an asset for oil and gas in the ground, but that discussion has focused on how to calculate the cost of those assets. With the level of development of geological methods, the quantity of oil and gas in a field can be measured reliably. A reliable unit price as of a current date, net of the lifting cost, also is known. The fair value of coal, iron, copper, silver, gold, and other minerals in the ground can be measured reliably in many circumstances. The fair value of those assets probably should be reported on the solvency statement.

Motion Pictures

Shortly after a motion picture has been released, its total audience can be estimated reliably, its ultimate revenue can be projected, and the fair value of this resource inflow can be calculated. These estimates are, in fact, used as a basis for a motion picture's rental charge. The fair value of those rents probably should be reported on the solvency statement.

Liabilities.   Current liabilities should be reported on the solvency statement as they are now reported on the balance sheet.

Pension and other post-employment liabilities, anticipated losses from litigation, deferred income taxes, and similar liability items resulting from the measurement of income should be reported as they are now. (Items that have a debit balance should be reported as assets.)

Liability for maturing bond issues should be divided between current and noncurrent liabilities, as it is now.

Convertible preferred stock poses a problem. Until it is converted, this item has no claim on the assets, but a claim will be created when the instrument is converted. A rule for this item is under discussion by the FASB.

Equity.   Shareholder equity should not be reported even though the fair value of common stock and preferred stock can be obtained from published sources. Reporting the total amount of stock at its market value would constitute circular reasoning since the market price is influenced by the financial statements.

Subsidiaries and Special Purpose Entities.   The assets and liabilities of consolidated subsidiaries should be reported. There are problems in the amounts for subsidiaries that are not 100 percent owned and for special purpose entities (SPEs) that are similar to the problem that exists with the current balance sheet.

Net Solvency. The balancing item net solvency is simply the difference between the reported assets and the reported liabilities. This is similar to the approach of measuring equity in a conventional balance sheet. Net solvency is an important number. A negative amount indicates that the entity is in trouble.

A "solvency ratio" will be more useful than the debt/equity ratio now calculated.

Notes. Nonfinancial items that appeared on the balance sheet, such as fixed assets, goodwill, and products resulting from research, should be reported in Notes to the financial statements. This is current practice for fixed assets and some intangible assets.

Ratios

Eliminating the balance sheet will require the development of new ratios. Instead of using the return on total assets, the new ratios may add the book value of assets (from the Note) to the financial assets. Alternatively, there could be a new ratio based on financial assets. The fact is that the book value of assets is neither their fair value nor their replacement cost. This ratio therefore has limited usefulness.

Regulated Industries

There is a special problem with regulated industries, especially those with sizable plant and equipment. Sales prices in those industries may be set to recover depreciation expense plus a profit. The depreciation amount is obtainable from the Notes, but there is no total asset number in a solvency statement; that number is needed to measure a return on assets.

One solution is to retain a balance sheet for those entities. In any event, the proposal for a solvency statement should not be shot down because of a problem that relates to only a few industries.

Arguments against a Solvency Statement

In this section I list arguments that may be made against the proposal and my responses to them.

A balance sheet is a useful check to auditors

A balance sheet reports that the Assets = Liabilities + Equity equation has been maintained, that the sum of debit amounts equals the sum of credit amounts. Without the balance sheet, there is no way to report this important fact.

Response

If there has been an error in making a journal entry to the accounts, the trial balance will identify it, and then the error will be corrected. Users can assume that the statements do not contain such an error.

The financial capital maintenance concept is ignored

Financial accounting should report the extent to which an entity has maintained its capital. There are two ways to measure this. The physical capital maintenance approach measures the extent to which performance produces resources that will replace all the assets. This approach is not feasible because the replacement costs of long-lived assets cannot be measured reliably. The other approach is called financial capital measurement. It does not attempt to measure the replacement cost of long-lived assets. The financial capital maintenance concept is sound. The existing balance sheet shows whether a company has at least maintained the amount that equity investors provided after the payment of dividends. This is an important way to judge management.

Response

Texts and articles describe the difference between the two approaches and show that the financial capital maintenance concept is more feasible. They do not go deeply into the soundness of this concept. For a company that has been in existence for only a few years, measurement of financial capital maintenance is useful. For a long-established company, its usefulness is doubtful. In such a company the long-lived assets are reported at their depreciated cost; the cost of assets procured in recent years would be larger. Some steel companies that have not kept the plant up to date may report excellent capital maintenance, but those firms cannot compete successfully with companies that have relatively new expensive plants.

Ratios and percentages would be lost

The debt/equity ratio and the return-on-equity percentage cannot be calculated from solvency statement data. These are important ways of judging the status and performance of a company.

Response

Equity on a balance sheet would be changed to net solvency on a solvency statement. The comparison of net solvency to liabilities is a more informative number than the comparison of equity to liabilities. Net solvency often is used in analyzing a company's ability to pay its bills even though there is now no required solvency statement. Return on equity has little meaning and indeed can be misleading for the reasons described above.

If users want to employ the current ratios, those ratios can be calculated easily by referring to the data in the notes to the financial statements.

Important information is omitted

The balance sheet contains important information about both long-lived and intangible assets. Relegating this information to Notes does not recognize its importance.

Response

Yes, data about these assets are important. In this book I do not describe the nature of those data. There are differences of opinion about whether long-lived assets should be reported at original cost, original cost less depreciation, replacement cost, or by another measurement method and whether the report should contain information about their condition.[7]

The balance sheet is an important educational tool

The importance of the accounting equation is emphasized in texts and in the classroom, and the balance sheet provides a good way to explain what the equation means.

Response

Users of financial statements are assumed to be knowledgeable about accounting. They already are familiar with the accounting equation. The balance sheet probably will continue to be discussed in texts and in the classroom as a tool for introducing this equation. It can be explained that the balance sheet once was used and is a good educational device even though it no longer is a published financial statement. Discussing the balance sheet items that are not reported on the solvency statement is a good way to explain the impossibility of measuring the fair value of certain items and therefore the undesirability of including those items on a conventional balance sheet.

The solvency statement does not report timing

Some liabilities will be due before the assets necessary to pay them off will be available. The solvency statement therefore in these circumstances is misleading.

Response

A status report necessarily applies to one moment in time. A time-phased statement would be three-dimensional and therefore cumbersome. The proposed statement uses present values as of the end of the accounting year. This statement does not reveal a possible financial crisis at an earlier time, such as the maturing of a large bond issue; management comments should call attention to that situation. If this item casts doubt on whether the entity is a going concern, the auditor should qualify his or her report. This is current practice.

Inventory measurement is inconsistent

The inventory of goods held for sale will be reported at cost unless the market value of the product is lower. This is inconsistent with the general approach to the measurement of balance sheet items. It recommends that assets be reported at their fair value (i.e., market value).

Response

Admittedly, this is inconsistent with the general rule. I accept the inconsistency because a gain from valuing inventory at market would anticipate revenue before it has been earned. This is inconsistent with the realization concept.

A compromise would be to report inventory at the lower of cost or market on the solvency statement but report revenue only when the product is sold. The solvency statement is not necessarily consistent with the income statement. My suggestion is debatable. I am concerned that this compromise would result in unnecessary questions from readers.

Use replacement costs for fixed assets

Although depreciated cost does not measure the value of plant and equipment, this category can be made consistent with the concept of measuring assets at their fair value by re-porting those assets at replacement cost. Replacement cost is in effect a measure of current value.

Response

I do not believe that replacement cost measures fair value. It as-sumes that the asset will be replaced by a similar asset, and this is by no means common. The asset may not be replaced at all, and if it is replaced, the new asset may be physically different.

Also, replacement cost as of the balance sheet date is not a likely estimate of what the replacement cost of an asset actu-ally will be even if it is replaced with a similar asset. The new asset may be better in several respects. Replacing computer components is an example.

In short, making reliable estimates of replacement cost usu-ally is not feasible, and even if a reliable estimate were feasi-ble, it would not be useful. The FASB experimented with the use of replacement cost, and it has abandoned that experi-ment for good reasons.

Depreciable assets are ignored

Depreciable assets and other fixed assets are necessary to the continued operation of an entity. Since a solvency state-ment measures whether an entity is likely to continue, these assets should be included in such a report.

Response

Although these assets are necessary, I doubt that this is a reason for including their book value in a solvency statement. Accounting usually assumes that an entity is a going concern;

the user's attention should be directed to any factor that makes this assumption unrealistic.

Fixed assets are treated inconsistently

The solvency statement omits depreciable assets, but the income statement includes them.

Response

Depreciation expense is a necessary element of the income statement. An entity has not earned net income if its revenue does not equal these and other expenses. The solvency statement numbers exclude these items.

There will be two reports

Users are accustomed to a balance sheet and will need considerable time to get used to a solvency statement. Therefore, at least during the transition period, both reports should be published.[8]

Response

Publishing two status reports with essentially the same financial information in different formats would be confusing.

A solvency statement requires too much work

Implementing the solvency statement will require considerable revision of accounting standards and extensive conversion to the new statement. The costs outweigh the benefits.

Response

A few accounting standards will have to be revised, but those standards relate principally to the format of the solvency statement. Changing the name of the document from "statement of financial position" to "solvency" is a minor inconvenience.

Adopting the solvency statement will have little effect on analyzing and booking individual transactions; most of the changes are in the totals. The annual changes in the Internal Revenue Code are time-consuming, but preparers and users understand the need for making those changes. Progress in accounting requires change.

Balance sheet misconceptions are unimportant

The argument for the proposal pays too much attention to the fact that balance sheet numbers are based on two different measurement bases. Informed users already know this.

Response

Accounting should do what it can to make the numbers understandable for *all* users. A solvency statement is an important step toward this goal.

Solvency should be included within the balance sheet

Rather than scrapping a statement that has served everyone well for hundreds of years, it would be better to keep it and identify solvency items by reporting them in a separate section of the balance sheet.

Response

This proposal is inconsistent with the basic reason for doing away with the balance sheet: that it is a misleading, incomplete statement of an entity's financial position.

Existing contracts require a balance sheet

Some contracts require the contractor to have a specified amount of owners' equity or one of its components. For example, a contract may prohibit paying dividends to shareholders if net worth is not at least a specified amount. These contracts will have no frame of reference if the balance sheet is deleted.

Response

The recent rules for reporting fair values affect items on the balance sheet that existed when the contract was sealed. Other changes in standards also may affect the balance sheet. The parties will amend the contract to incorporate these changes. The existence of a solvency statement is only one reason for making such amendments.

The cash flow statement is enough

The cash flow statement can be used as a report on solvency. Another statement is not needed.

Response

The cash flow statement reports flow during the period, not status at the end of the period. Therefore, it is not a substitute for a solvency statement, which is a report on status at the end of the period.

Negative equity is not revealed

A solvency statement does not reveal the fact that an entity may have negative equity. This is important information.

Response

Negative equity has little meaning. The amount of actual assets may be understated greatly for the reasons given above, and the actual equity may be positive; there is no way of telling whether this is so. Many start-up entities, especially dot-com companies, have little or no equity in their initial years; they are building market share that will turn into profits if they succeed. Negative equity may prohibit the payment of dividends, but those entities ordinarily do not pay dividends. By contrast, insolvency is a serious situation that can lead to legal actions on the part of bondholders or other investors.

Prior references

The text has given inadequate attention to prior writings.

Response

Most of the literature on solvency refers to the usefulness of solvency information. I have mentioned only the few instances in which a solvency statement was suggested.

Inadequate evidence

This book does not provide the evidence that a scholarly article should use as a basis for conclusions.

Response

I know of no way to devise a test that would provide evidence for the use of a solvency statement. The alternative is a statement that reports all items at their fair value. However, the fair value of nonmonetary items is not known and cannot be estimated. Inability to measure fair value exists in all companies that have substantial fixed assets such as plant and goodwill.

Darwin's *The Origin of the Species* is not an acceptable scholarly statement by current standards: It does not have adequate statistical evidence.

Summary

The balance sheet has served a useful purpose for almost 500 years. The emphasis on fair value rather than cost in the last 20 years has made the balance sheet obsolete.

The solvency statement *is* useful. Even today, solvency assets and liability totals are more widely used than are conventional total assets and total liabilities in litigation and auditing. I recognize that it will be difficult for accountants and users of accounting information to change to a new statement. It will take time, but I believe that the transition will involve relatively few problems and that an acceptable solution can be reached for each of them.

Notes

[1] In the landmark case *Eisner v. Macomber* in 1920, Charles Evans Hughes, later to become Chief Justice, summed up in his brief to the Court this view: "It is of the essence of income that it should be realized. . . . Income necessarily implies separation and realization. . . . The increase in the value of lands due to growth and prosperity of the community is not income until it is realized." The Supreme Court accepted that view and defined income as "not a *growth or increment* of value in the investment, but a gain, a profit, something of exchangeable value in the investment, proceeding from the property, severed from the capital. . . ."

[2] Concepts and Standards Research Study Committee, "The Realization Concept," *Accounting Review*, April 1965.

[3] For example, paragraph 29 of CON 5 states, "Important uses of information about an entity's financial position include helping users to assess factors such as the entity's liquidity, financial flexibility, profitability and risk." There is no mention of solvency.

[4] The Joint Working Group of Standards was founded in 1997. It consists of nominees of accounting standards setters in Great Britain, Japan, Germany, five Nordic countries, the United States, and the International Accounting Standards Committee.

[5] Admittedly, this creates a problem. The Internal Revenue Service will not allow LIFO for tax purposes unless it also is used for the balance sheet. The solution may be a note that describes the difference.

[6] "The Conceptual Framework and Accounting for Leases." By Dennis W. Monson in *Accounting Horizons*, September 2001: Vol. 15, #13. Page 177. This article referred to *Leases: Implementation of a New Approach*, Hans Nailor and Andrew Lennard, February 2000. Pages 24–25.

[7] *Abacus*, Vol. 36, no. 2, 2000 "Options for Infrastructure Reporting" describes this information.

[8] Heath proposed this solution. In other respects his analysis is excellent. *Heath* (1978) "Financial Reporting and The Evaluation of Solvency," New York, 1978. AICPA.

4

THE INCOME STATEMENT

In recent years the Financial Accounting Standards Board (FASB) has issued several standards that deal with the measurement of net income. This chapter focuses on one issue: the recognition of equity interest. This choice is consistent with the purpose of the book, which focuses on basic issues that are not currently on the FASB's agenda.

Equity Interest

I propose that the cost of using equity capital be reported in the same way the cost of using debt capital is reported.[1] This cost should be labeled "equity interest."

Accounting should treat interest cost the same way economics treats it. In economics "interest" refers to the cost of using capital. Accounting defines the term differently in two fundamental respects. First, in financial accounting interest refers only to the cost of using *debt* capital; accountants do not record a charge for the use of *equity* capital. Second, in financial accounting the total interest cost for a period is reported as an item on the income statement. By contrast, economics treats interest as a component of the cost of each of the assets and expense items that use capital, similar to the way labor and other cost items are treated. By "capital" I mean the amount of debt and equity capital listed on the right-hand side of the balance sheet.

I propose that accounting adopt the concept of interest used in economics. Specifically, interest on the use of both debt and equity capital should be accounted for as an item of cost—the cost of using capital—and should be reported in the same way other items of cost are reported:

- The cost of goods manufactured should include an interest charge for the use of capital tied up in the plant and equipment involved in the manufacturing process, and inventory amounts should include that interest cost.
- The cost of assets held for sale or use in future periods, such as petroleum reserves, should include the interest cost of holding those assets.
- The cost of new plant assets should include interest on the capital used during the construction process (once an asset has been put into productive use, no further interest cost would be accumulated for it).
- Interest costs that exceed the amounts included in these asset items should be charged as an expense of the period.

These rules correspond to the generally accepted accounting principles (GAAP) for other items of cost, such as labor. The labor used on products becomes part of their cost and is included in their inventory amounts. Labor used to construct plant is part of the cost of the plant. Other labor costs of the period are reported as general and administrative expenses.

This proposal is not new. Early in the twentieth century a similar proposal was advocated vigorously and debated hotly. The debate subsided in the late 1920s, and except for discussions among a few accounting theoreticians in more recent years, the business community has given practically no thought to the possibility of revising GAAP to incorporate such a proposal.

Conceptual Foundation

Economics describes principles that govern the operation of a business. Financial accounting measures and reports the results of business operations. One would expect the principles of financial accounting to be consistent with the principles of economics unless there were good reasons for a divergence. Those who seek to justify such a divergence should bear the burden of proof.

The inconsistency between the accounting treatment and the economics treatment of interest is taken for granted by a great many people. Actually, two basic accounting concepts—the entity concept and the cost concept—*do* support the recording of interest as a cost.

In the nineteenth century accounting was governed by what is called the proprietary concept: Assets were *owned* by the proprietors, and liabilities were *owed* by the proprietors. With that concept there was no point attempting to record the cost of using equity capital separately from the profit earned by a business since both the capital charge and the profit "belonged" to the proprietors.

With the development of publicly owned corporations the basic idea of accounting shifted from the proprietary concept to the entity concept; the corporation was viewed as an entity entirely separate from its proprietors. This entity obtained its capital from two principal sources: Debt capital came from creditors, and equity capital came from shareholders either directly or indirectly as retained earnings. Equity capital therefore became just another source of funds. Under these circumstances it would seem appropriate to measure the cost of using the equity capital, which is supplied by outside investors, just as it is appropriate to measure the cost of using debt capital, which also is supplied by outside parties. From the standpoint of the entity, each type of capital is a resource furnished by an outside party. (The profitable operation of the business is a source of capital. Shareholders permit this capital to remain in the business rather than being distributed to them as dividends.)

Under the cost concept, assets initially are recorded at their cost. Costs that expire in an accounting period are called expenses. Net income is the difference between revenues and expenses. If interest is in fact a cost, it should be recorded as an element of the initial cost of assets that require the use of capital and should attach to the asset amount until an asset becomes an expense. For example, manufactured goods should be recorded in inventory at amounts that include the interest cost of the capital employed in the manufacturing process, and this interest cost should be one element of expense in the period in which those goods are sold.

Cost measures the quantity of resources that are used for some purpose. In manufacturing a product, for example, a company uses a resource called labor, which is measured by salaries, wages, and related fringe benefits. It uses another resource called material, which is measured by material costs, and it uses resources that collectively are called services, which are measured by utility costs, rentals, and similar items. A company also uses capital; that is, it obtains funds, which it uses to acquire assets. Those who have that capital, whether lenders or shareholders, will not furnish it to a company unless they anticipate receiving a reward for doing so. Capital therefore has a cost; it should be called interest. Interest represents the cost of using someone else's capital, just as rent is a cost of using someone else's building.

Those who maintain that interest should be treated differently from the other elements of cost, such as labor, material, and services, should be prepared to demonstrate how interest is fundamentally different.

Management Accounting

Although interest on total capital is not recorded as a cost in financial accounting, the concept that the use of capital has a cost, which should be explicitly recognized, is well accepted in the internal accounting used by management.

In the 1960s increasing use of present value focused on the cost of using capital, both debt and equity. The present value concept was used principally in cases in which a single payment made now was compared with a stream of resource inflows over a period of time. For example, consider a proposed investment of $100,000 in a new machine that reduced production costs. The stream of savings was discounted at an earnings rate to arrive at its present value.

Before the 1950s there were several ways to analyze problems of this type. One was the accounting method that used an estimated income statement for about half the life of a machine; this was thought to approximate the present value of the machine. Alternatively, one could examine whether the investment in the machine would be recovered through cost savings over a period of time. This was called the payback method. A third method involved trial and error: What discount rate made the stream of savings equal to the investment? These approaches were crude; they did not account for the present value of the stream of savings accurately.

Discounting these inflows at the cost of capital was known to be the correct approach, but it required the use of the following formula:

$$\text{PV of } n \text{ periods hence} = 1/(1 + i)^n$$
$$\text{where } n = \text{number of years}$$
$$i = \text{interest rate per year}$$

This formula required the use of a calculator, but few students in the 1950s had access to a calculator. Students did have slide rules, but they gave only rough answers after one moved several slides. The civil engineering profession had tables that gave present values, but those tables had a maximum discount rate of 8 percent.

Professor Joel Dean, author of the text *Capital Budgeting* (1951), doubted that the effort to calculate present value was worthwhile. He wrote:

Discounting the stream of capital earnings to take account of the diminishing value of distant earnings is an integral part of the theory of capital value. It introduces complications of measurement, however. When the economic life of assets is short or fairly uniform, when earnings estimates are necessarily rough, and when uncertainty rises steeply in the distant future, this refinement is not worth its complexity cost.

Present Value Tables. In 1955 Chuck Christenson of the Harvard Business School persuaded the Harvard Computation Laboratory to compute complete present value tables on its machine, which was one of the largest in the world. A few hours of effort produced two tables: (1) "Present Value of $1 received N years" and (2) "Present Value of $1 received annually for N years." Both were for up to 40 years and 50 percent interest rates.

United Shoe Machinery, 1955. In 1955 a federal court ordered the United Shoe Machinery Corporation to sell machines that it previously had leased. This required that some multiple be applied to those lease rates. I headed the team that arrived at those selling prices by using present value techniques, and the court accepted those numbers. This was the first major litigation involving present value that I know of.[2]

FAS 34

In the 1960s and early 1970s many articles were published that dealt with the cost of using capital. They were based primarily on the increased use of this concept in management accounting. In 1973 Philip L. Defliese, managing partner of Coopers & Lybrand and a past chairman of the Accounting Principles Board, developed a proposal along those lines (see Exhibit 2).

In addition to allowing for interest, Defliese proposed adjusting the depreciation charge so that the sum of depreciation and interest (adjusted for income tax effects and, if appropriate, major maintenance and renovation expenditures)

Exhibit 2. Statement of Operations Proposed by
Philip L. Defliese (millions of dollars)

Income Operations:		
Sales		$453.9
Less Cost of sales	$308.4	
Other expenses	119.7	
Provision for income taxes	21.9	450.0
Profit from operations (after taxes)*		$3.9
(per share of common stock: $1.30)		
Capital Operations:		
Imputed interest on net investment in facilities and operating assets (capitalized or charged to income operations)		$21.1
Less Interest paid to creditors and lessors (after tax)	$1.6	
Dividends on preferred stock	0	1.6
Net return on equity capital investment		19.5
(per share of common stock: $6.50)		
Total Income and Capital Operating Results		$23.4
Less Dividends paid to common stock ($3.00 per share)		9.0
Current year's capital formed and retained		$ 14.4
Prior year's capital formed and retained (Bal. Jan. 1)		126.4
Total Capital Formed and Retained		$140.8

* This is net operating income *after* all charges for the holding costs of facilities, including interest on capital invested and depreciation.

Source: Adapted by permission of Philip L. Defliese.

would be approximately the sum for each year of the asset's life. This total annual cost for the use of a purchased asset would correspond closely to the amount of annual payments that would be made for the same asset if it were leased. Since the annual interest cost decreases over time as the amount of capital tied up in a project becomes smaller, leveling the annual cost requires that depreciation be charged at increasing annual amounts. The annuity method of depreciation results in such a schedule of increasing charges.

Defliese's proposal, with examples, is developed carefully in a paper submitted to the Securities and Exchange Commission (SEC). It differs in some details with the procedure I describe here, but the end result is basically the same, and I wholeheartedly support it. Present value was on the agenda of the Accounting Principles Board when it was superseded by the Financial Accounting Standards Board in 1973.

The Institute of Management Accountants suggested that this topic be added to the FASB's agenda. In 1974 the SEC became concerned with accounting for interest cost when it noted that an increasing number of nonutility registrants were adopting a policy of capitalizing interest as part of the cost of certain assets. Charles Bowsher, the SEC's chief accountant, told me informally that he would oppose any effort to count equity interest as a cost. On June 21, 1974, the SEC issued a release that proposed a moratorium on adopting or extending a policy of capitalizing interest by registrants other than public utilities and asked the FASB to develop a standard on this topic. The FASB added the topic to its agenda.

In 1979 the FASB issued Financial Accounting Statement (FAS) 34, "Capitalization of Interest Cost." The basic error in the FASB's approach was its definition of "capital." The management accounting articles and practice defined that term as including both debt capital and equity capital. The FASB documents included only interest on debt capital, which it defined as "interest recognized on obligations having an explicit interest rate." It stated that interest on equity capital was "imputed interest," which implied that the cost of using equity capital was not a "real" cost. This is a strange implication because dictionaries define an "imputed" cost as a cost that has to be allocated or estimated; there is no implication that it is not a "real" cost.

Although FAS 34 was titled "Capitalization of Interest Cost," it includes only part of the interest on equity capital. It stated that some debt capital was specific to a project and that the interest on it was part of the interest cost. Other debt interest was to be estimated by the proportion of debt capital involved in the project. The total interest amount in the period that was charged to assets could not exceed the total amount of debt interest in that period. FAS 34 permitted the use of interest on both debt capital and equity capital in public utilities but in no other entities. Other refinements to this general idea were included in FAS 7, 42, 58, 62, and 127.

FAS 34 was adopted by a vote of four to three. The board members in the minority said that the cost of assets should not include *any* interest cost: Interest was a general cost of a business. The compromise, as is so often the case, disappointed both sides. Proponents of equity interest were unhappy about its omission. Proponents of the status quo were disappointed that any "unreal" number was recognized.

Paragraph 49 of FAS 34 stated that "some accounting board members believed that it may be appropriate at some time in the future to consider whether the cost of equity capital should be recognized within a framework for financial reporting that continues to be based primarily on historical cost." This has not happened, and I believe the time has come.

Implications of the Proposal

Recording interest as a cost would have a greater impact on the numbers reported in an income statement than has any change since the introduction of depreciation accounting. It also would have implications for the use of accounting information in discussions of public policy, taxation, rate regulation, contract pricing, and other government rules. It would increase the harmonization of management accounting information with financial accounting information. Its effect in these areas is described briefly below.

Implications for Financial Accounting.   If the economic facts of interest were recorded in the accounts, readers of financial statements would understand the status and performance of a business more clearly.

With few exceptions, notably public utilities and the other companies mentioned above as well as the partial recognition of equity interest in FAS34, a building constructed by a company's own personnel now appears on the books at a lower cost than does an identical building constructed by an outside contractor. This is the case because companies do not include equity interest cost on a self-constructed building but do include an allowance for the use of their capital in the price of a building constructed by an outside party. There is no logical reason to omit interest costs for self-constructed buildings and include them for purchased buildings.

The longer an item remains in inventory, the greater its actual cost is to the company. The amount of this additional cost is immaterial in companies with rapid inventory turnover, but it is important in companies that hold inventories for significantly long periods, such as inventories of tobacco and distilled liquor. Because accounting does not recognize the cost of those inventories, that cost is understated.

The return on equity capital that a company earns consists of two elements: interest and profit. In current practice those elements are combined in the single number labeled "Net Income." Although a company's production and marketing activities contribute to the generation of income, accounting recognizes the return only as of the time the product is sold. In effect, therefore, accounting reports that all return on capital is earned by the marketing organization and none is earned by the production organization. If interest were recorded as a cost incurred throughout the operating cycle, the offsetting credit would show a corresponding return on capital earned in each period of the cycle.

If equity interest cost were accounted for separately as an expense, the bottom-line amount on an income statement would be smaller than it is now. Net income would show how much an entity earned over and above a charge for the cost of the capital it used. That number would be a good measure of performance because an entity that has not generated enough revenue to cover all its costs, including the cost of using capital, has not performed satisfactorily. This net income amount would not be affected substantially by the relative amount of debt and equity in a company's capital structure. In current practice the debt/equity ratio has a great influence on the Net Income amount.

Additions to shareholders' equity during a period would come from two sources: the charge for equity interest and Net Income. The sum of those two amounts would differ somewhat from the current Net Income amount because of timing differences arising from the interest cost that is embedded in assets. Over a period of years, however, that total amount of shareholders' equity would not be affected materially by the proposal.

Public Policy Implications.   Many government agencies use the accounting information they obtain from business firms. Including interest as an element of cost would facilitate the work of those agencies. The process of rate setting by regulatory agencies would be simpler and more straightforward. Price controls could be designed on the principle that prices should provide a fair return on the capital employed.

There are advantages to adopting a similar principle for income tax calculations. The fact is that interest expense on debt is tax-deductible but no deduction is allowed for the corresponding cost of using equity capital. Because interest on debt capital is tax-deductible, borrowing is better than using equity capital. These discrepancies would be removed if a reasonable interest cost on equity capital were allowed as a business expense.

Currently, the public is not convinced that if a business is to survive, it must earn enough to cover the cost of using all its capital. This message would come through clearly if the cost of using equity capital were labeled for what it is: a real cost. Although a few people may claim that any amount of profit above the minimum cost of capital is unwarranted, the general public undoubtedly would regard the Net Income amount as an indication of good performance, which is essential in the usual economic system. In any event, the articles that now "prove" that profits constitute a large fraction of the sales dollar would not be valid.

As a related point, confusion about why profit margins, expressed as a percentage of sales, vary so widely among companies of various types would be lessened. One important reason for these differences is the difference in the amount of capital employed; the facts would be clearer if interest were counted as an element of cost.

Harmonizing Financial Accounting and Management Accounting

No principle requires that the internal accounting information used in managing a business be consistent with the financial accounting reports prepared for outside parties, but such consistency has at least two advantages. First, it reduces the need for two sets of books. Second, it lessens the misconception that financial accounting numbers are "real" numbers and that numbers constructed according to other principles are "soft" or even "phony." Many people—probably the majority—do not believe that equity interest is a real cost despite what they read in economics books and despite their awareness of the fact that capital cannot be obtained if the shareholder is not expected to be rewarded for furnishing it. Financial accounting would be more credible if it treated equity interest as a real cost. Consequently, within a business there would be increasing acceptance of profit-center performance measurements that incorporate a charge for the capital employed. Recognizing interest costs in calculating economic order quantity, determining appropriate inventory levels, outsourcing, optimizing working capital amounts, and product pricing also would have greater credibility.

Implementing the Proposal

Recording interest on both debt and equity capital as a cost is as critical as recognizing it. There are two practical problems in doing this. The first and more important problem is choosing a way to measure the interest cost of using equity capital. The second is the largely procedural problem of deciding how to incorporate interest cost in the accounts.

Measuring the Cost of Using Equity Capital. Measuring the cost of using debt capital usually is thought to be easy; the amount is stated in the loan agreement. Measuring the cost of using equity capital, by contrast, often is considered impossible. Neither conclusion is accurate.

Measuring the interest cost of debt capital is difficult in a number of situations. Specifically, problems arise in measuring the interest cost on bonds that are sold at a discount or at a premium, adjusting for the call premium and unamortized discount when a bond issue is refunded, measuring the cost of convertible bonds sold at a yield that is significantly less than the going rate of debt interest, and imputing a cost to certain debt instruments in which the interest and principal components are not shown separately. In all these situations FASB pronouncements require an approximation of the true annual interest cost. Calculating this cost can be complicated. Nevertheless, the accounting profession tackles these problems, and it is increasingly willing to use complicated procedures in order to report the true interest cost of using debt capital.

Admittedly, there is no precise way to measure the interest rate applicable to equity capital. No one has described a method of making a precise measurement that is widely accepted as valid, generally applicable to companies, and sufficiently objective to be used as a basis for financial reporting, and no one is likely to do so. Nonetheless, businesspeople do make judgments that implicitly involve such a rate. They often use a number that approximates the average interest rate for both debt and equity. Because the rate for debt interest is calculable, the rate for equity interest can be deduced from this average.

Since the nineteenth century the estimated cost of using capital has been an element in the calculation of rates for regulated public utilities, in analyses involving proposed capital investments, and in companies that use a required earnings rate, a required rate of return, or a comparable number. Companies that use the residual income method of measuring divisional performance must compute a "capital charge" as one element of a division's cost.

The approaches used for these purposes provide a good starting point for devising a principle to measure interest cost for financial accounting purposes. However, some special considerations must be taken into account. Specifically, (1) the method must apply to all types of businesses, (2) the method must be reasonably objective; that is, the rate cannot depend on management's unverifiable estimate, and (3) the calculation must be relatively straightforward. The following suggestions offer a feasible approach:

- Companies should calculate the interest cost of debt capital the same way they do now.
- For financial accounting purposes all companies should use an interest rate on equity capital that is specified directly by the FASB or arrived at objectively by a method prescribed by the FASB. This rate should represent a minimum equity interest cost; that is, it should be somewhat lower than the actual cost of equity capital. It might be called the *prime equity rate.*
- The prime equity rate could be either the current rate or the rate that existed at the time that increment of capital was acquired, as is currently the case in calculating the interest cost of debt capital. However, it is likely that the prime equity rate will be a fixed percentage of the known debt rate.

Accounting Procedures. If one accepts the fundamental proposition that interest is a cost that should be treated in the way other elements of cost are treated, most of the accounting procedures can be determined easily by analogy with other cost elements. Those procedures are summarized below:

- Each entity should develop an overall interest rate. That rate should be the weighted-average of the firm's debt rate and its prime equity rate in a given year.
- Except in unusual transactions in which there is a stated mix of debt and equity capital, this overall rate should be applied to the capital employed for various cost objectives in order to determine the interest cost applicable to those objectives.
- The interest cost of capital assets used in the manufacturing process should be assigned to products in the same way that depreciation on plant and equipment is assigned.
- The cost of self-constructed plant and equipment should include the interest cost of the capital assets used to construct the plant and equipment and the interest cost of other capital that is tied up during construction.
- The cost of acquired plant and equipment should include the interest cost of advance payments and progress payments.
- Any interest cost for a year that is not assigned to cost objectives should be treated as a general expense of that year.
- The credits for these charges should be made in an interest pool account. This account should be debited for the actual cost of debt interest—adjusted for its tax effect—and the amount of equity interest, calculated at the prime equity rate.
- The amount of equity interest should be credited to retained earnings.

Suggestions for the Transition

The change proposed here is substantial, has many ramifications, and requires an extensive educational process before its import can be well understood. For these reasons a gradual transition to the new method should be developed. Among the various possibilities, starting with selected items in specific industries is perhaps the most workable. Two suggestions follow:

- Include interest as an element of inventory cost in companies that hold inventory for long periods. Examples include the standing timber of companies that own timber, the oil reserves of petroleum companies, and inventories of tobacco, distilled liquor, and other products that are aged for several years.
- Include interest as an element of cost in self-constructed buildings and equipment as required in FAS34, but at the total interest rate.

Federal Cost Accounting.   In Defense Procurement Circular 107 the Cost Accounting Standards Board permitted the inclusion of equity and debt interest costs on capital assets used for cost-type contracts. It considered but has not adopted a provision to include interest on current assets as a cost.

Income Taxes.   The relevant congressional committee has considered the acceptance of equity interest as an allowable tax expense but has not adopted this concept. The effect would be a substantial decrease in the amount of corporate income taxes, and this has not been acceptable.

Literature.   There have been a few articles, mostly in foreign periodicals, recommending that financial accounting adopt equity interest. The New Zealand government takes account of equity interest in its system.

There are two principal reasons why financial accounting has not adopted this general idea. First is the mistaken notion that arriving at the equity interest amount would be too subjective. Second is the heavy hand of tradition. The first argument has been addressed above. Unfortunately, as is the case with many proposals, acceptance requires support from many influential people.

Other Income Statement Problems

The FASB has a number of studies under way relating to accounting for the measurement of net income. My comments on these topics obviously would be premature, but I comment on a few of them below.

Stock-Based Compensation

There are many different forms of stock options, but in a common one a person, usually an employee, is given approval to purchase a specified number of common stock shares at a specified price. On the issuance date the exercise price is almost always higher than the market price of the stock, and the recipient would be foolish to exercise it. Its value rises if the exercise price is lower than the market price at some later date. Exercise at that future date is an expense valued at the difference between the option price and the market price on that date.

A company can account for a stock option in either of two ways. One is the "intrinsic value–based" method, which is essentially the current market price of the stock.

The other is the "fair value–based" method, which is an estimate of what the market value of the stock will increase to in the future. This is referred to as the Black-Scholes method.

The fair value described in Appendix B (¶ 273) of FAS123 is a formula derived by estimating the "exercise price and expected life of the option, the current price of the underlying stock, its expected volatility, the expected dividends on the stock and the current risk-free interest rate for the expected life of the option." This formula often is used to estimate the fair value of debt securities, but the components applied to the future behavior of common stock are rough estimates at best.

The prices of Black-Scholes securities fluctuate around an average, whereas the price of common stock is estimated to increase in the future, but the amount is a wild guess.

The problem is that no one knows what the market will be in the future, and therefore, that value is uncertain. There have been many efforts to arrive at that value, but all of them involve an estimate of what will happen in the future.

In 2002 the FASB was working on the problems associated with stock-based compensation to employees. This is a complicated topic, and I do not attempt to suggest rules. In International Standard 19 (IAS 19), the International Accounting Standards Board states that it does not address "stock-options."

At the end of 2002 the Conference Board and the International Accounting Standards Board were studying this problem.

Special Purpose Entities

A Special Purpose Entity (SPE) is an entity that is created by another organization but whose assets and liabilities are not reported in the consolidated financial statement of that organization. It is highly limited by the criteria described in detail in paragraph 26 of FAS125, "Accounting for Transfers and Servicing of Financial Assets and Extinguishing of Liabilities." Transactions involving SPEs are described in many other paragraphs of FAS125. If experience shows that those requirements do not close the previous loophole for not reporting SPEs, additional requirements will be needed.

Balanced Scorecard

There is a considerable body of literature about the use of what is called a "balanced scorecard." (This is a new name for key variables.) The literature reports various ways of measuring performance and includes both financial accounting information and nonfinancial information such as investment in employee training, employee morale, more effective service quality, and customer satisfaction. My analysis is limited to financial statement information and therefore does not discuss the nonfinancial aspects.

Definition of Net Income

Net Income, the "bottom line" of an income statement, is the most important number in financial accounting. Strangely, the FASB does not define it. One can deduce from FASB literature that Net Income is the net effect of almost all changes in equity other than transactions with equity investors. The few items that do *not* affect Net Income are listed in various pronouncements. Those pronouncements say what Net Income is not rather than what it is.

A definition should distinguish between items that affect Net Income and items that do not. The latter items are either additions to assets (i.e., capitalized) or direct entries to equity. The definition of "development costs" is an example of a definition that currently is controversial.

The line between income statement items and direct entries to equity is now drawn by listing the items that will not appear on the income statement. A generalization that would help determine which items to add to or delete from this list would be welcome, but there may be no satisfactory way to state such a generalization.

Analysis of Income

The International Accounting Standards Board (IASB) uses the term "income" and a synonym, "net profit or loss." Its definition of income (IAS 97) has two components: (1) "profit or loss from ordinary activities" and (2) "extraordinary items." In Accounting Principles Board (APB) Opinion 30 "extraordinary items" are defined as "events *and* transactions that are distinguished by their unusual nature and by the infrequency of their occurrence." The IASB does not distinguish between extraordinary elements that are a component of Net Income and extraordinary elements that affect equity but are not a component of Net Income.

The G4 + 1 group published two reports on income measurement.[3] This group consists of standards setters from Australia, Canada, New Zealand, the United Kingdom, the United States, and the IASB. It has been disbanded, and its members now are associated with the IASB. Those reports recommended some useful changes in the measurement of financial performance, but none of the recommendations have become rules.

The definitions of income statement items cannot be entirely objective. For example, goods that are shipped to the buyer's warehouse *are* revenues if the customer intends to sell or use those items. They *are not* revenues if there is an understanding that the shipment will become the owner's asset again shortly after the period ends. This practice is used to sweeten the current period's Net Income. Framing a rule that prevents overstating income for this type of transaction may not be possible. Proper treatment requires determining management's intention and therefore is subjective. The auditor should consider the facts carefully and decide whether the transaction actually results in revenue in the current period.

Operating versus Nonoperating

As APB 30 states, an income statement has two sections. One section reports what loosely can be called "operating" revenues and expenses. It is divided into pretax and after-tax components. The other section reports all other income statement items; those items are described as "extraordinary," "nonrecurring," or "nonoperating." Because several ratios refer to "operating" revenues and expenses, defining those elements is important. "Operating" is not a good name because it does not have a clear meaning.

FAS 95 defines operating activities as activities that are neither investing nor financing. Interest expense is a financing activity and therefore is not an operating activity, according to this definition. FAS 95, however, relates to the cash flow statement, and the definitions in that statement are not quite the same as those for income statement items. The text should reconcile the different definitions.

The general meaning of "operating" is that it relates to the normal ongoing activities of an organization. This meaning can be clarified by referring to other standards. For example, "operating revenues" relates to goods delivered or services performed in the period; several standards refer to the time period. Similarly, "operating expenses" describe resources consumed in the period during the course of general activities. Since some gains and losses are classified specifically as nonoperating, it follows that other gains and losses are operating.

Certain financial transactions are without question operating. Working capital—current assets less current liabilities—relates to operating activities. To the extent that receivables and inventory are not financed by payables to suppliers and employees, they must be financed by either debt or equity. This use of funds has a cost, just as the use of depreciable assets has a cost. The cost is an operating cost and was discussed at length in an earlier section of this chapter.

The use of financial resources results in a cost. Many marketing and manufacturing activities use financial resources, and those activities have a cost. Financing may be affected by the magnitude of product development activities, the amount spent on advertising, the size of inventory, credit policies, outsourcing decisions, and so on. Most people would agree that these are operating activities and that financing them involves a cost.

According to the FASB, nonoperating items of an income statement include events that are unusual, infrequent, and material; events associated with discontinued operations; the effect of a change in accounting principles; and adjustments made to Net Income in the prior period that were omitted from that income statement or were reported inaccurately. An example of an adjustment to Net Income is a lawsuit that was settled for an amount significantly different from what was reported in the prior period (APB Opinion No. 3, FAS4, FAS 16, FAS 64).

Operating income is an important component of Net Income. There are 366 references to "operating income" in the FASB standards and 154 references relating to "operating profit," but neither item is defined, nor is a distinction made between them. (Perhaps they have the same meaning.)

Individual Items

Individual income statement items are now classified as revenues, gains, expenses, or losses. This four-way classification is unnecessarily complicated. Gains are a form of revenue and losses are a form of expense, and so only two categories are needed. Using only two categories simplifies the presentation, eliminating the need to draw a line between revenues and gains and another line between expenses and losses. Reducing the number of categories does not change the need for prescribing the treatment of gains and losses, as is done currently.

Rules for recognizing and measuring individual items are a perennial problem. Accountants discover a loophole that permits them to book a transaction in a way that increases Net Income, and the FASB or the SEC then devises wording that will close the loophole or at least reduce its size. Recording revenue from a sale that actually was not a sale, as was mentioned above, is a current issue. Unfortunately, the SEC and FASB rules for closing this loophole are not exactly the same. The Enron SPE fiasco is an example of a loophole used in a situation that turned out to be erroneous.

If a transaction affects both the balance sheet and the income statement, the proper income statement treatment should govern how the transaction is reported. The offsetting item on the balance sheet is for the same amount even if it results in a peculiar asset or liability. As was noted above, the entry for deferred taxes is an asset.

Unlike items that are reported on the balance sheet, some income statement items are properly reported at cost rather than fair value even though fair value can be measured adequately. Examples are uninsured losses from theft, disappearance, and acts of nature. They are reported at cost because if the entity has recovered the cost of those items, it has broken even.

Inventory markdowns and plant costs that cannot be recovered are properly expenses of the period in which those losses are identified, but appreciation in these assets is not recognized. This is in accordance with the conservatism concept.

The fair value of expense amounts for pensions and other postretirement benefit obligations incurred in the year usually are measurable. These are the amounts that would be paid to an insurance company or another outside party that provides for the benefits. The calculation uses the present value of the future payments. Occasionally, the amount owed may change because legislation or the inflation assumption has changed. The amount that an outside party would charge to provide for these changes is the amount that should be reported. These practices are stated in the current standards. They are mentioned here only to clarify the point that the income statement correctly includes them in the calculation of Net Income.

There should be more explicit rules for some items. For example, current standards permit any depreciation method that is "systematic and rational." Only four paragraphs in the FASB's thousands of pages of standards are devoted to depreciation. By contrast, 93 paragraphs address earnings per share.

Net Income can apply to both business and nonprofit organizations, whereas "earning" and "profit" are terms that apply only to business.

The sections of an income statement are arranged in a hierarchy; therefore, some numbers are the sum of lower-level numbers. The intended hierarchy should be maintained. The most obvious accounting sin is using the word "income" when something else is meant. Income is always a *difference* between revenues and expenses. "Interest income" should be "interest revenue." Interest is as much revenue as is sales. (The Internal Revenue Service makes the same error.)

"Revenue" is not a correct term for additions to capital. Amounts received from shareholders are not revenues; neither are capital contributions in nonprofit organizations.

FAS 116 and 117 use "revenue" in some sentences for contributed capital items and list these items on the same line as revenue. This treatment is incorrect. "Revenue" relates only to resource inflows from activities of the current period. In other places these standards refer to capital inflows as "restricted support." Paragraph 209 of FAS 116 defines "restricted support" as a form of revenue. It is no more revenue than are receipts from the issuance of stock in a business.

A report of inflows and outflows is called a "Statement of Activities" in nonprofit organizations. It is given a longer title such as "statement of revenues, expenses, and changes in fund equity" by the Governmental Accounting Standards Board. These differences in terminology imply that there are differences in substance between the revenue and expense standards of nonprofits and governments and the standards of business accounting. This implication is incorrect. In all three types of organizations the flows are revenues, expenses, gains, and losses.

Revenue Measurement

The FASB is currently studying its definition of revenue. There are many complications. For example, Merck was criticized by the SEC for counting as revenue $12 billion worth of consumer copayments. A consumer copayment is the amount paid by a customer that is part of the sales price of a specific item. Actually, if this amount is counted as Merck revenue, it is accompanied by an equal amount of expense. The Merck net income is therefore a lower percentage of revenue than the amount would be if those transactions were omitted.

Summary

This chapter deals with the measurement of income and the classification of the components that enter into that measurement. There should be a better definition that separates income statement items from other changes in equity. The classification of the components of income needs to be clarified.

Notes

[1] This section is a condensed version of my book *Accounting for the Cost of Interest* (Lexington, Mass.: Lexington Books, D.C. Heath and Company), 1975.

[2] FASB Concepts Statement No. 7, "Cash Flow Information and Present Value in Accounting Measurement" (2000), describes and illustrates several methods of working with present value.

[3] These reports are *Reporting Financial Performance: A Proposed Approach*, September 1999, whose principal author was Kathryn Cearns, and *Reporting Financial Performance: Current Developments and Future Directions*, January 1, 1988, whose principal authors were L. Todd Johnson and Andrew Lennard.

5

STATEMENT OF CHANGES IN EQUITY

Chapters 3, 4, 5, and 6 of this book each relate to one of the required financial statements. This chapter describes the statement called "Statement of Changes in Equity." However, this classification is unfortunate.

In 1997 the Financial Accounting Standards Board (FASB) issued Financial Accounting Standard (FAS) 130, "Reporting Comprehensive Income." That standard requires a financial statement that reports comprehensive income, but not necessarily with that name. In my opinion this requirement is both unnecessary and misleading. It is unnecessary because the same information can be reported in the statement of changes in equity. It is misleading because "comprehensive," meaning large in scope or content, would appear to be more important than Net Income.

The discussion in this chapter is limited to the items of performance that are included in financial statements, but those items and the several possible financial statements are defined differently in various FASB pronouncements. This illustrates the need for an overall revision of accounting standards to eliminate unnecessary differences. The FASB is making a study of these matters.

Background

"Clean-Surplus" Concept

Before 1967 there were two schools of thought about reporting financial performance. Some people favored the "current operating performance" concept, believing that the income statement should focus on operating activities. Entities with this view charged or credited amounts for nonoperating activities directly to equity. Other people believed that charging nonoperating outflows, such as losses from the sale of securities or the sale of fixed assets, charged directly to equity "sweetened" the bottom line of an income statement because it moved an expense item from that statement to equity. They favored the "all-inclusive" or "clean-surplus" concept, which supported their belief that almost all transactions relating to performance in the current period should enter into the measurement of Net Income.

APB Opinion 12

Accounting Principles Board (APB) Opinion 12 is the 1967 "omnibus" opinion of the Accounting Principles Board. Paragraph 10 on capital changes states:

> When both financial position and results of operations are presented, disclosure of changes in the separate accounts comprising stockholders' equity (in addition to retained earnings) and of the changes in the number of shares of equity securities during at least the most recent annual fiscal period and any subsequent interim period presented is required to make the financial statements sufficiently informative. Disclosure of such changes may take the form of separate statements or may be made in the basic financial statements or notes thereto.

This was the first standard that required a report of changes in equity in addition to the measurement of Net Income.

There was no list of the items that should be included in such a report.

APB Opinion 19

APB Opinion 19, "Reporting Changes in Financial Position," was issued in 1971. It pretty much settled the controversy mentioned above in favor of the clean-surplus concept. It did so by listing a few items that should be charged or credited directly to equity and requiring the inclusion of all other items in the measurement of Net Income. From time to time a few items have been added to this list, including the correction of errors in the preceding income statement, certain foreign currency transactions, a change in the market value of hedging contracts, a new loss on pension liability, and unrealized holding gains and losses on certain securities transactions.[1]

APB Opinion 20

APB Opinion 20, "Accounting Changes," also issued in 1971, dealt with accounting changes. It required that the current year's measurement of Net Income include Net Income changes of prior years that resulted from actions taken in the current year. Those transactions included changes in accounting principles and the effect of an error that changed the Net Income of prior periods. They were reported in the line above Net Income on the income statement.

APB Opinion 15, "Earnings per Share," which was issued a year earlier, excluded these prior-period adjustments from the measurement of earnings. In all other respects earnings and Net Income have the same meanings as in APB Opinion 20. Therefore, in those relatively rare situations in which a prior-period adjustment occurred, the definition of earnings differs from the definition of Net Income. This is why the number is labeled "earnings per share" rather than "Net Income per share."

FAS95

Although FAS95 (1987), "Statement of Cash Flows," mostly concerned cash flows, its first paragraph stated without explanation that the report of changes in equity required in APB Opinion 19 was superseded. Nevertheless, many companies continued to publish a statement of changes in equity. The items contained in this report are those required by the various standards listed above.

CON 3

Accounting rules are described in standards, not in concepts statements. Most practitioners pay little attention to concepts statements, the purpose of which is to guide standards setters.

Concepts Statement (CON) 3, "Elements of Financial Statements of Business Enterprises," issued in 1980, contained a diagram titled "Transactions and Events That Change Equity of Business Enterprises." This diagram is reproduced in Exhibit 3.

The concept of Net Income is not even mentioned in CON 3. CON 3 describes intermediate components or measures resulting from combining these elements and asks, Which, if any, should be emphasized to the extent of being the bottom line of a financial statement? However, CON 3 does not answer this question. The stated justification for that omission is that "ways of providing information about various sources of comprehensive income are matters of display that are beyond the scope of this Statement."

CON 3 describes revenues, expenses, gains, and losses in some detail, but the description relates entirely to those four items, which are components of Net Income. It says nothing about items, such as those listed in APB Opinion 19, that affect equity but do not enter into the calculation of Net Income.

I understand the reason for this strange omission is that the board could not agree on a definition or even the name that should be given to the bottom line of the income statement.

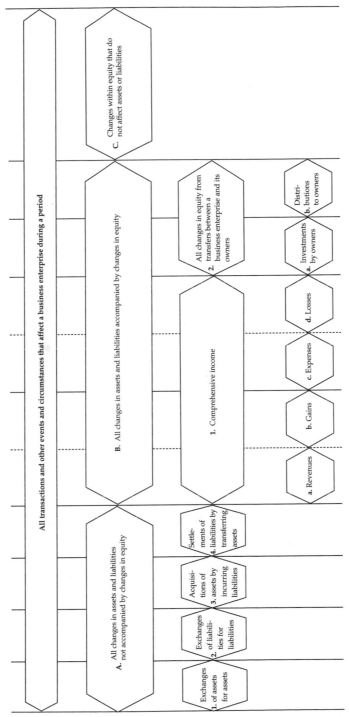

Exhibit 3. Transactions and Events that Change Equity of Business Enterprises

CON 5

The distinction between items that should be included in the measurement of Net Income and items that should be carried directly to equity is described in CON 5, "Recognition and Measurement in Financial Statements of Business Enterprises" (1984). A table in paragraph 44 shows that comprehensive income is the sum of three components: earnings, cumulative accounting changes, and other nonowner changes in equity. "Earnings" in this statement is similar to Net Income for a period in current practice.

Earnings and Net Income have almost the same meaning. The single difference is that Net Income includes an adjustment for the "cumulative effect on prior years of a change in accounting principles" and earnings does not.

One financial statement was a report on Net Income (or earnings), and another was a report of comprehensive income. The report on Net Income (or earnings) included revenues, expenses, gains, and losses, and the report on comprehensive income included Net Income plus all other nonowner changes in equity.

CON 6

CON 6, "Elements of Financial Statements" (1985), dealt with two topics. One was a word-for-word copy of the former CON 3. The other was a discussion of nonprofit organizations. The two topics were identified separately throughout CON 6. CON 6 contained the same diagram that is reproduced in Exhibit 3.

FAS130

FAS 130, "Reporting Comprehensive Income," issued in 1997, requires one financial statement that reports Net Income and its components and another financial statement that reports comprehensive income. The report on comprehensive income includes all other nonowner changes in equity. The report on comprehensive income is said to be new but actually is similar to the report required in APB Opinion 19.

The impetus for developing FAS 130, according to its appendix, was a paper published by the Association for Investment Management and Research (AIMR), an association of financial analysts. That paper was entitled *Financial Reporting in the 1980s and Beyond.*

The appendix further states (paragraph 41) that Robert Morris Associates, another financial analyst association, "indicated support for what it referred to as an all-inclusive income statement at a 1995 meeting of the Board by stating that 'Net Income should include the effect of *all* of the current period's economic transactions and other activity of the entity.'" This broad definition of Net Income goes against all current usage, and I doubt that it had much support.

With the exception of the unrealistic recommendation of Robert Morris Associates, most responses to the Exposure Draft referred to in the report recommended a report similar to that in APB Opinion 19. They certainly did not favor the report on comprehensive income that is the subject of FAS 130.

The board countered that argument by referring to APB Opinion 12, which briefly alluded to this issue. However, Appendix A to FAS 130 did not even mention APB Opinion 19, which dealt with it specifically and at length.

The Exposure Draft that became FAS 130 was issued in June 1996. Public hearings dealing with the treatment of financial instruments, as well as comprehensive income, were held in November 1996 and early 1997. FAS 130 was issued in June 1997. Deliberation was much shorter than was the case for other important standards. Some of the topics discussed in the 1996 and 1997 hearings had not been acted on as of 2003.

Defects

A New Statement Is Not Needed

An obvious question is, Why didn't the FASB simply resurrect the report required by APB Opinion 19, amended to include additional items that are direct changes in equity as required by more recent pronouncements? Although APB Opinion 19 is inconsistent with CON 3 and CON 6, it is entirely consistent with the more recent CON 5. Many companies continue to publish this type of report even though it has not been required since the issuance of FAS95 15 years ago. It is a straightforward listing of nonowner transactions that are direct entries to equity.

There are many indications in the appendix to FAS130 that respondents to the exposure draft preferred this solution.

Comprehensive Income Is Misleading

A second question is, Why use the term "comprehensive income"? The very thorough index to accounting concepts and standards published by the FASB makes *no* mention of "comprehensive income" other than references in FAS130, CON 5, and CON 6. By contrast, a similar search for "Net Income" turned up 1,384 references.

The likely answer is that the FASB was trying to salvage its invention, the term "comprehensive income." Having a term that is described at length in concepts statements but is not used in practice is embarrassing. Although the FASB tried hard to sell comprehensive income in FAS130, the evidence indicates that it is unlikely to succeed. The definition in CON 6 is an error.

The term "comprehensive income" implies that the items excluded from Net Income are in fact "income." This makes no sense. Those items go directly to equity because they are *not* income. "Income" is the difference between revenues and expenses.

The word "comprehensive" implies that comprehensive income is more important than Net Income; in fact, the opposite is the case. Net Income generally is accepted as the important "bottom line," and many ratios and other comparisons use it. I know of no ratios or other bases for comparison that use the comprehensive income number.

The AICPA annually publishes in *Accounting Trends and Techniques* a summary of the format and content of 600 companies. Its 1996 report—eight years after the repeal of APB Opinion 19—stated that 448 of those 600 companies continued to publish a statement of changes in equity or a similarly titled document. Not one company used the term "comprehensive income."[2]

Despite these defects, there has been little opposition to FAS 130 in the literature. The reason seems to be as follows: The report is easy to prepare, so why fight it?

A definition that includes all nonowner changes in equity would be feasible but would serve no useful purpose. Box B1, entitled "Comprehensive income," includes revenues, gains, expenses, and losses. The net amount of those components is the Net Income for the period and would be so listed on the Income Statement. However, no mention is made of gains and losses that are not involved in the measurement of Net Income but that do affect equity. These are the items referred to in APB Opinion 19 and its successors. Box B2 is labeled "All changes in equity from transfers between a business enterprise and its owners." Box B1 plus Box B2 accounts for *all* changes in equity.

This diagram is obviously incorrect. Revenues, expenses, gains, and losses are the components that make up Net Income, but equity also is changed by other nonowner transactions, such as those listed in APB Opinion 19. Neither the diagram nor the accompanying discussion distinguishes between items that are properly included in the measurement of Net Income and items that should be carried directly to equity. Also, there is no indication in Exhibit 3 and the accompanying text that such a distinction should be made.

The box labeled "Comprehensive Income" should be divided into two boxes. One should refer to the four elements of revenues, gains, expenses, and losses, and the other should refer to items that affect equity but not Net Income. The omission of such a box is an error.

FAS 130 correctly describes a statement of comprehensive income. It states that comprehensive income includes both the items that are included in Net Income and the items that are included in other additions to equity. These items are covered in FASB statement Nos. 12, 52, 80, 87, and 115. The FASB does not mention the fact that Statement 130 supersedes APB Opinion 19. Moreover, the FASB does not mention that the Net Income components are reported separately from the other items mentioned above. This omission results in the error in CON 6, which does not mention any of these items.

Remedy

The statement of changes in equity should be resurrected, and the statement of comprehensive income should be scrapped.

The statement of changes in equity contains all the information about nonowner changes in equity required in the statement of comprehensive income except for the few items that have been added to the list since its publication. Also, its title does not mislead users into believing that comprehensive income is of primary importance.

The statement also includes information on transactions with equity investors that are not required in any other statement, and so there is no need to report that information separately. Paragraph 55 of CON 5 requires a report of investment by and distribution to owners. This information should be included in the statement of changes in equity.

The "direct changes in equity" class is now defined by the

list of items included in it. If feasible, there should be a general definition that will be used in considering proposed additions to it. It should not open the door wider than it is now. Admittedly, reaching agreement on such a definition may not be feasible.

A committee of the American Accounting Association has commented on the report by G4 + 1.[3] It endorses the principle of a single financial statement but raises many questions about the details of the proposal.[4]

In other chapters I have argued against those who support the status quo, but in this case I join them. Net Income is the most important single number in financial accounting. Granted, it does not have a precise definition. It reports an entity's financial performance, taking account of almost all increases and decreases in equity. Items that distort the report of performance are excluded because they are even less related to what has happened than are items reported as "extraordinary." There are only a few such items, and their treatment is debatable. Is an unrealized loss on securities unrelated to performance, or does it reflect management's inability to identify the probable decrease and sell the security before it occurs?

I believe that standards setters should clarify the line between items that enter into the measurement of Net Income and items that do not and should retain the basic idea of "Net Income."

An analyst who differs from a rule on the measurement of Net Income can easily adjust the reported bottom line. Most users want such items to be identified as a signal that the entity's income statement should be examined more carefully— a signal derived from the price/earnings ratio, comparison with prior periods, or other variables.

G4 + 1 Proposal

The G4 + 1 group has proposed a single statement should report all nonowner changes in equity. It would have three sections:

1. The results of operating (or trading) activities
2. The results of financing and other treasury activities
3. Other gains and losses

   The group's report does not define the three sections, stating that such definitions require further discussion and analysis. In general, however, the third section—other gains and losses—would include items now reported in the "extraordinary" section of the income statement, plus other nonowner changes in equity now reported in a statement of changes in equity or the new statement of comprehensive income. This sometimes is referred to as a "black hole." There would be no Net Income number.

   The group believes the income statement contains a mixture of items that have different implications for the prediction of cash flows and the other purposes for which the income statement is used. Also, there are differences in the way income is measured in member countries. For example, dividends are reported as a reduction in income in some countries, and performance measurement includes an item for the revaluation of fixed assets in some countries.

   This case for a single report is not convincing. It obscures the important message conveyed by two reports that almost all nonowner changes in equity are reported on the income statement. A few changes are not associated with the activities of the current period. To include them on the income statement would distort the message that an income statement conveys. They are listed in a separate statement. This statement is relatively unimportant; it simply lists these items.

Conclusion

The treatment of nonowners' changes in equity has a long and convoluted history. The remedy is to have two reports: one measuring Net Income and the other listing changes in equity. Owners' changes in equity might be reported separately.

Many comments on this topic refer to ambiguities or other minor defects in the income statement. These defects should be corrected, but doing away with a separate report would be throwing out the baby with the bathwater.

Notes

[1] For a detailed list, see paragraph 28 of FAS 130.

[2] If someone claims that this is the case because the comprehensive income statement was not required at that time, this is a tacit admission that companies will not use this term unless they are forced to do so.

[3] The G4 + 1 group consists of representatives of standards-setting organizations in Australia, Canada, New Zealand, the United Kingdom, and the United States, plus a representative from the International Accounting Standards Committee. Its 1999 report was titled "Reporting Financial Performance: A Proposed Approach."

[4] American Accounting Association, Financial Accounting Standards Committee, "Response to the Special Report of the G4 + 1" (2000).

6

THE CASH
FLOW STATEMENT

This chapter tells a story of misunderstanding. Beginning in the 1950s, many companies prepared a funds flow statement that reported the sources and uses of funds during an accounting period. That statement was codified in 1971 by Accounting Principles Board (APB) Opinion 19, "Reporting Changes in Financial Position."

Sixteen years later the Financial Accounting Standards Board (FASB) published Financial Accounting Standard (FAS) 95, "Statement of Cash Flows." Despite the difference in the titles that statement dealt with the same flows as those discussed in APB Opinion 19. It is, however, defective in several respects. I suggest that FAS95 be superseded by a statement similar to APB Opinion 19.

Background

Early Years

A financial statement for reporting changes in working capital was introduced in the 1920s. It gained widespread acceptance in the accounting literature largely as a result of the ef-

113

forts of Professor H. A. Finney, the author of leading accounting texts and the editor of the Students' Department of the
Journal of Accountancy. Finney therefore exerted considerable
influence on accounting issues at that time.

For example, the first edition of *Accounting: Text and Cases*
(1955), which I coauthored, contained a section on the funds
flow statement similar to what was proposed later in APB
Opinion 19.

In 1963 the Accounting Principles Board issued APB Opinion 3, "The Source and Application of Funds." Its content was
similar to that of APB Opinion 19, which was issued eight
years later.

APB Opinion 19, "Reporting Changes in Financial Position," focused on funds, specifically, two types of funds: working capital and noncurrent items. The opinion listed changes
in each item of working capital and gave the sources of noncurrent funds and the uses of those funds.

Accounting faculty found that constructing a funds flow
statement was a useful exercise. It described the changes in
balance sheet items in an accounting period by using the difference between the items on the beginning and ending balance sheets. "Sources" were increases in current liabilities,
and "uses" were increases in current assets. For example, if
inventory increased in the accounting period, that meant
more cash was tied up in inventory. If accounts payable increased, that meant vendors were in effect providing a source
of funds.

The funds flow statement made the important point that
even if an entity increased Net Income during a period, there
might be a problem if cash was not available to finance the
additional inventory and accounts receivable associated with
that growth. The bankruptcy of the W. G. Grant Company illustrated that problem. Over a period of several years that
large retailer grew rapidly, in size, which was reflected in increasing net income. But its inability to finance the related
current assets led to disastrous financial difficulty. A similar
problem led to the bankruptcy Kmart.

In addition, the statement helped explain the difference between cash accounting and accrual accounting.

This information was available in the balance sheets for the beginning and the end of the period and in notes for some of these items.[1] The statement answered the following questions:

- How much cash did the entity's normal ongoing operations provide?
- In what other ways were significant amounts of cash raised?
- Was the entity investing enough in new plant and equipment to maintain or increase capacity and replace old facilities with more efficient ones?
- Was the entity reinvesting excess cash in productive assets, or was it using that cash to increase dividends or even to retire some of its common stock?
- To what extent were the company's fixed assets being financed by internally generated cash?
- For cash obtained from outside sources, how much was from debt, and how much was from equity?[2]

The flows listed in APB Opinion 19 were called "funds flows." Articles and letters to the FASB thereafter referred to "cash flows." The examples contained in those materials showed that the authors were referring to the same items that were listed in APB Opinion 19 despite the different label.

The FASB put the funds flow statement on its agenda in 1980 and issued a discussion memorandum, "Reporting Funds Flows, Liquidity, and Financial Flexibility." Note that the reference was to funds flows. It held hearings in May 1981.

Six months later, in November 1981, the FASB issued an exposure draft of a proposed concepts statement, "Reporting Income, Cash Flows, and Financial Position of Business Enterprises." Note the change to cash flows. This became Concepts Statement No. 5 (CON 5), issued in December 1984.

In 1984 the Financial Executives Institute strongly encouraged the FASB to focus on "cash flows" in the development of

CON 5. In 1985 and 1986 a task force met with groups of financial analysts, financial executives, small business representatives, and others to discuss cash flows. The task force was replaced in March 1986 by the Advisory Group on Cash Flow Reporting.

In July 1986 the FASB issued an exposure draft, "Statement of Cash Flows." That statement was discussed at meetings with representatives of the Financial Analysts Federation, the Financial Executives Institute, the National Association of Accountants, and Robert Morris Associates.

In November 1987 the board issued FAS95, "Statement of Cash Flows." The statement had only 34 paragraphs but was accompanied by 85 paragraphs on its basis for conclusions. It was adopted by a vote of four to three. The three dissenters explained their positions at length.

This standard was amended by FAS102 in 1988, which was adopted by a vote of six to one, and by FAS104 in 1989, which was adopted by a vote of five to two. In all cases the dissents were a red flag about the soundness of the requirements, although dissents are to be expected on complicated topics. I believe this was the longest, most thorough discussion of a topic until that time. In addition to the meetings mentioned above, the FASB received more than 700 letters on the topic.

As a participant in some of these activities, I can testify that much of the discussion was complicated by semantic differences, especially the difference, if any, between the meaning of "funds" and that of "cash."

Defects

FAS 95 is different in three respects from APB Opinion 19: It (1) recommends reporting by the "direct" method, (2) permits only literal cash flows, and (3) requires cash flows to be classified as operating activities, investment activities, or financing activities.[3] For the reasons discussed below, I believe that these changes are unsound.

Direct versus Indirect Methods

APB Opinion 19 reported the changes in the current accounting period on working-capital accounts: current assets and current liabilities. Those changes reflected either the uses of cash or the sources of cash. The analysis started with the Net Income of the period. To this was added depreciation and any other expenses that did not require cash. The sum was the amount of cash generated by income-producing activities. Some of that cash might be tied up in an increase in a current asset. An increase in the inventory account meant that there was less cash available for noncurrent purposes, such as the acquisition of fixed assets. Conversely, a decrease in a current asset was a source of cash because less cash was tied up in that asset. The effect was the opposite for current liabilities. An increase in accounts payable meant less cash was needed. A decrease meant that more cash was used to finance working capital and that that amount of cash could not be used for another purpose.

The FASB preferred a different method: It reported the amount of cash increases and decreases from various sources. Cash collected from customers was a source of cash, and cash payments to suppliers and employees were uses of cash.

The board called its preferred approach the "direct method." It labeled the APB approach the "indirect method" because it did not measure directly the operating receipts and expenditures that caused cash to change.

The differences between the two methods are illustrated in Exhibit 4.

The direct method reports the amount of cash received from customers and the amount of cash disbursed to suppliers and employees and for income taxes. These are the items that affect working capital. In the indirect method, the report shows that operating activities generated cash flows and that those flows were larger than the amount reported as Net Income because some of the expenses included in the measurement of net income did not require the use of cash. The effect

Exhibit 4
Cash Flow Statements — Operating Section
for year ended 2002
($ thousands, condensed)

A. Direct Method

Cash received from customers	$13,300
Minus cash paid to suppliers	6,400
Minus cash paid to employees	5,480
Minus income tax paid	800
Equals cash inflow	$620

B. Indirect Method

Net income	$1,600
Depreciation	320
Subtotal	1,920
Changes in working capital	
Plus increase in accounts receivable	1,080
Plus increase in inventory	610
Minus increase in accounts payable	305
Minus increase in wages payable	408
Minus increase in taxes payable	80
Cash provided from operations	$897

on cash of the changes in working-capital items is described in the next section. The net amount is the amount of cash generated by operating activities. This amount ends up as a change in the cash account. Other sections of the statement showed how that cash was used.

Remedy

Superficially, the direct method of measuring anything seems superior to an indirect method. This is not the case with the cash flow statement, where the indirect method actually is more informative. For example, the direct method reports cash received from customers. So what? This item does not help analysts learn about the need for cash. The indirect method reports the change in accounts receivable during the year. If the change is consistent with the change in sales volume, it is to be expected. If it is more than the amount expected because of sales volume, it indicates a potential problem with collecting receivables, with changing credit terms, or with other areas that warrant attention. The direct method does not permit such an analysis.

Moreover, although "direct" implies that the desired number is easily obtainable from the accounting system, the opposite is true. Many transactions that do not literally involve cash actually are relevant to the sources and uses of current assets and liabilities. Cash debits and credits to accounts receivable take account of returns, exchanges, errors, write-offs, and other events that affect the actual change in accounts receivable in addition to receipts from customers. Identifying the cash items relevant to inventory is even more complicated. In the indirect method the numbers are taken directly from the balance sheet.

Many respondents to the exposure draft favored the direct method because it sounded good. I suspect they were unaware of the analysis that can be made with numbers derived from the indirect method and the bookkeeping complications involved in using the direct method.

Among the 600 corporations whose financial statements were summarized in the 1997 American Institute of Certified Public Accountants (AICPA) study *Accounting Trends and Techniques*, 590 (98 percent) used the indirect method. That statistic does not reflect a sluggish response to a new FASB requirement; FAS95 had been in effect for six years. It means the companies believed that the indirect method was more informative.

Three Sections

FAS95 divides cash flows into three types of activities: operating, investing, and financing. The section on operating activities is essentially the same as that in APB Opinion 19. The classification of other flows as either "investing" or "financing" is both confusing and unnecessary. The FASB justified this treatment by referring to paragraph 20 of CON 5: "Classification in financial statements facilitates analysis by grouping items with similar characteristics and separating items with essentially different characteristics." Although this is a good generalization, it does not work here. As an example,[4] the APB Opinion 19 approach would list the following as items relating to a new plant (in thousands of dollars):

Expenditure for new plant	$10,000
Sale of old plant	500
Bond issue	(8,000)
General funds	$1,500

Classifying these transactions as either "investing" or "financing" is arbitrary. For example, FAS95 classifies "proceeds from the sale of facilities" as an investing flow, but those proceeds could just as well have been classified as part of the cash used in financing a new plant.

I believe that most companies prefer the approach they used before the FAS95 requirement. Some actually report a funds flow statement even though this is no longer required. The fact that over 90 percent of large companies prefer the indirect method is compelling both for the use of that method and for FAS95 in general.

Limitation to Literal Cash Flows

APB Opinion 19 was about flows of "funds." The FASB correctly maintained that "funds" is a vague term. Although "cash" is a specific term, limiting the statement to literal cash flows means that some financial transactions must be excluded. An important example is the issuance of common or preferred stock in payment for the acquisition of plant. FAS95 requires that these transactions be reported in a separate note to the financial statements rather than in the text of the cash flow statement. Issuing common or preferred stock is as much a source of cash as is the issuance of debt. The statement would be more informative if it included these sources.

Remedies

Indirect Method

The standard should require the use of the indirect method rather than the direct method. The direct method need not even be mentioned. Most of the complexity of FAS95 results from attempts to solve the problems that arise from using the direct method. The FASB should note the fact that almost all companies have disregarded its recommendation.

The complexity of FAS95 and the subsequent changes made by FAS102 and 104 are adequate reasons for issuing a new pronouncement on cash flows. The FASB should resurrect the former APB Opinion 19 as a starter in such a revision.

Title

Even though the statement is not literally limited to cash flows, it can be called a Cash Flow Statement as a response to the objection many people have to the word "funds." It should include the issuance of common or preferred stock as payment for an acquisition of plant even though that transaction does not literally involve cash. These resource inflows can be explained by stating that they may be thought of as obtaining cash from issuing the securities and immediately using that cash to pay for the plant acquisition. FAS95 does not permit this transaction in the body of the statement. Therefore, the statement does not tell the complete story about the acquisition.

Operating Section

The operating section should be retained because it shows why Net Income is different from increases in cash. This section should be reorganized to emphasize changes in working capital, that is, the difference between current assets and current liabilities. Increases in working capital must be financed by noncurrent sources: either retained earnings or the issuance of new bonds or stock. Exhibit 4 provides an abbreviated description.

Combine Investing and Financing

Investing and financing activities should not be classified separately. Instead, preparers should be encouraged to report the nonoperating flows in whatever format is most informative. International Accounting Standards Committee (IASC) International Accounting Standard 7 has an adequate way of doing this; an example is shown in Exhibit 5.

Exhibit 5
Cash Flow Statement — Nonoperating Section
for year ended 2002
($ thousands, condensed)

Construction of Plant A:		
Cash disbursed	$7,205	
Less proceeds from borrowing	5,000	
Receipts from sale of old plant	650	
Net cash for Plant A		$2,855
Disbursements for other capital assets		890
Proceeds from other borrowing		550
Dividends paid		400
Net cash for nonoperating activities		$2,115

Other Topics

In its lengthy consideration of the cash flow statement the board addressed a number of topics that will be relevant in the proposed revision. They should be retained. CON 7, "Using Cash Flow Information and Present Value in Accounting Measurements," (February 2000) provides some suggestions.

Notes

[1] In this statement I refer to the balance sheet. The same analysis applies to the solvency statement described in Chapter 3.

[2] These questions are taken from the tenth edition of Robert N. Anthony, David F. Hawkins, and Kenneth A. Merchant, *Accounting: Text and Cases*, 1999, The McGraw-Hill Companies, Inc., Burr Ridge, Illinois.

[3] These items are described in H. Nurnberg, "Inconsistencies and Ambiguities in Cash Flow Statement No. 95," *Accounting Horizons*, June 1993, pp. 60–75.

[4] This example consist of my interpretation of the text and examples from FAS95. Others may disagree, but the point is still valid.

7

NONPROFIT
ACCOUNTING

The rules for financial accounting in nonprofit organizations are basically defective. Most important, they treat all transactions as part of a single system rather than separating current contributed capital transactions from other transactions. Before the adoption of current Financial Accounting Standards Board (FASB) rules, most nonprofit organizations made such a separation in their accounting systems. The FASB's current rules do not state that the proper conceptual separation take place, thereby creating the potential for misleading financial information. Moreover, the FASB's failure to fine-tune the existing rules despite widespread criticism from the professional accounting community is a defect in the rule-making process itself.

The FASB added nonprofit accounting to its agenda in 1977. Its first document, Concepts Statement No. 4 (CON 4) (1980) made one important point but was otherwise uninformative. Concepts Statement No. 6 (1985) was defective. Its nonprofit standards currently in use—93 (1987), 99 (1988), 116 (1993), 117 (1993), and 124 (1995)—are all defective. This chapter explains why.

Background

In the 1970s accounting standards for nonprofit organizations were stated for several nonprofit industries. Those standards were published in three American Institute of Certified Public Accountants (AICPA) Audit Guides for nonprofit industries and in a Statement of Position.[1] The standards differed from one another in many respects, primarily because they were developed by different people. They had the common characteristic that all of them distinguished between current transactions and contributed capital transactions. Contributed capital transactions are changes in equity that do not affect Net Income. They are similar to but in some respects different from transactions that affect equity capital in a business corporation.

In 1977 the FASB commissioned me to identify the nonprofit issues it should deal with if it accepted jurisdiction. It assembled a group of 53 advisers, the largest group ever to work on an FASB project. There were experts on all nonprofit industries who provided important information and commented on drafts of the report. My final report, *Financial Accounting in Nonbusiness Organizations: An Exploratory Study of Sixteen Conceptual Issues*, was published in 1978. As the title suggests, it identified 16 issues and some of the pros and cons related to each one. It did not suggest how those issues should be resolved.

In retrospect, I think this approach did not go far enough. The FASB's staff prepared a discussion memorandum that was based on the report and held meetings in Washington, San Francisco, and Chicago in the fall of 1978 to discuss it. However, the 16 issues were not referred to in any subsequent document, and no reasons were given for discarding or ignoring them. A standards-setting body such as the FASB wants proposals to chew on, even though obtaining majority opinions from the large committee would have been difficult. My report did not recommend changes to the accounting rules.[2]

CON 4

The FASB's first substantive document following my report was CON 4, "Objectives of Financial Reporting by Nonbusiness Enterprises." It was issued in December 1980.

Paragraph 4 of CON 4 contained the sentence "Financial reporting must distinguish between resource flows that are related to operations and those that are not." This should have suggested the proper framework for nonprofit accounting, but this distinction has been made only in paragraph 23 of FAS117, where it is an optional subset of the FASB's Statement of Activities.[3]

CON 4 also describes three distinguishing characteristics of nonbusiness organizations:

1. They receive contributions.
2. Their purpose is not to earn a profit.
3. They do not have transferable ownership interest.

Ironically, these three characteristics are more indicative of *similarities* than of differences between for-profit and nonprofit organizations. At the same time, they fail to clarify several important differences. The other 63 paragraphs in CON 4 do not describe anything that requires unique nonprofit accounting standards. I do not recommend that CON 4 be amended; it does no harm.

Contributions for capital purposes are unique, or almost unique, to nonprofit organizations. Contributions for current purposes, in contrast, are revenues of the current period and should be accounted for just like other types of revenue.

Although nonprofit organizations do not have the purpose of earning a profit, their financial performance should be measured by the difference between revenues (including gains) and expenses (including losses), the same measurements used in business. In a business income statement this difference is labeled "Net Income." This is an appropriate name for the bottom line of the Income Statement in a nonprofit organization. Standards setters who prefer another term want to emphasize differences; I want to emphasize similarities.

With regard to ownership, the fact that nonprofit organizations do not have transferable ownership interests means only that they do not have accounting transactions for ownership. This does not lead to a different model any more than the fact that some business organizations do not have preferred stock leads to a different model for them.

CON 4 asserts that the contributions received by nonprofit organizations are "nonreciprocal transfers" because donors do not receive assets of equal value in return. This is true but irrelevant. The only relevant difference is that nonprofit organizations have two types of contributions. Some contributions (e.g., grants and annual fund drives) are revenues; they are no different from sales revenue inflows in a business. Others (e.g., endowment, contributed plant, and museum objects) are contributed capital. They add to equity, just as do inflows of capital from shareholders in a corporation.

Contributions, such as grants, received for work that is to be done in a future period are liabilities until that work is done. They are the same as advance payments in a business.

Exposure Draft on "Elements"

In July 1983 the FASB issued an exposure draft (ED) on nonprofit "elements." It proposed a new element that it called "contributions." This disregarded the distinction between the two types of contributions: current and capital. The ED was criticized strongly, and after much discussion the staff conceded that "contributions" as an element would not fly. This approach was abandoned.

CON 6

For the next six years the nonprofit task force met, working papers were written, and another exposure draft was issued that was widely criticized and abandoned. In early 1985 the board instructed its staff to issue a nonprofit accounting concepts statement by December of that year. Consequently, the FASB issued an exposure draft in September.

Michael Hebert of Bryant College analyzed the 1,193 responses to this exposure draft—a difficult task—and found that 92 percent of the respondents disagreed with it. Nevertheless, this ED, with minor revisions, became the nonprofit section of CON 6, "Elements of Financial Statements," issued in December 1985, just 3 months after the ED was issued, compared with the average interval between an exposure draft and the final document for the preceding five concepts statements of 13 months. Because of this rapid transition from ED to CON, CON 6 became an excellent example of the waste that results from haste. In this case the waste was a concept paper that was inconsistent with a framework that distinguished between current and contributed capital transactions.

Although the accounting models used before 1985 by nonprofit industries differed from one another in certain details, most of those models distinguished between current transactions and contributed capital transactions. The FASB model replaced that distinction with three "classes" of equity: unrestricted, temporarily restricted, and permanently restricted. Transactions are assigned to these classes solely on the basis of the explicit request of contributors.

There is no precedent in the literature or in practice for this three-class model or any sound conceptual underpinning for it. The previous classification had two categories, not three, and the classification was based on a contributor's intent even if that intent was only implicit. This classification led to much more informative financial statements than did the new FASB model.

The three-class FASB model was invented to solve a minor problem: the treatment of grants. From all accounts, the staff concluded that receiving grant funds to undertake a project did not create a liability because the organization might not be obligated to return the money if it did not do the specified work. If the grant was not liability, what was it? The only other place to book the credit amount was to equity. However, other contributions to equity were for assets that had a long life, such as plant and endowment. Those entries were basically different from the additions to equity resulting from revenues and expenses, and so the staff created the temporarily restricted class.

Logically, this led to the two other classes, one on either side: unrestricted and permanently restricted. The unrestricted class included all grants and contributions that were explicitly unrestricted by the grantor or contributor simply because the term was "unrestricted."

Organizations that have significant amounts of contributions to endowment and/or plant must classify much of those contributions as unrestricted. As a result, they tend to overstate the "Change in Unrestricted Net Assets," which is the FASB's name for Net Income. Many unrestricted contributions, especially bequests, are so large that they obviously were not intended for current purposes. In the previous model they had been characterized as "board-designated endowment." In the current model they must be treated as unrestricted revenue. The same is true for donated plant.

Since most transactions in nonprofit organizations are the same as those in business accounting, the FASB could have used the relevant business standards and limited its work to a brief statement and to standards that were unique to nonprofits. It didn't do this.

Criticism

Criticism of the FASB model has been unusually strong and has not abated. For example, in 1995 an AICPA committee asked for comments on a proposed "Audit and Accounting

Guide for Not-for-Profit Organizations." There were 154 responses. Typically, respondents to an exposure draft of this type limit their responses to issues on which they are asked to comment; they do not challenge the standards which an accounting guide is intended to help implement. By contrast, more than 30 respondents to this exposure draft made recommendations that would require a change in nonprofit standards.

Many other criticisms came from community foundations. The new standards require a drastic and undesirable change in the way those organizations treat contributions.

The strongest objections came from eight arts organizations (mostly symphony orchestras). Their letters had a similar theme, but they were by no means form letters. The Boston Symphony Orchestra (letter 74) stated that it planned to publish unaudited financial statements that separated current transactions from other transactions, that it also would prepare audited statements in accordance with the new standards, and that it would file them away because no one would want to see them.

Other specific criticisms were as follows:

- Seventh-Day Adventists (letter 18): "Application would be impractical or impossible."
- Community Foundation of Greater Flint (letter 25): This "will hamper the growth and management of community foundations."
- The Dayton Foundation (letter 38): The requirements are "burdensome loads."
- Virginia Society of CPAs (letter 43): These are "arcane accounting requirements that have little or no benefit."
- First Church of Christ, Scientist (letter 107 [facetiously]): This "will make a dramatic improvement in our financial position overnight."
- Baptist Foundation of Texas (letter 110): This is "adding a degree of complexity and costs that far outweigh the benefits."
- Community Foundation of St. Joseph County (letter 113):

"These changes in accounting standards will cause far greater confusion and misinterpretation than they correct."

• Johns Hopkins University (letter 141): There is "dismay over standards that require recording and reclassification of transactions into 'classes.'"

In the "Basis for Conclusion" section for each of its standards, the FASB usually discusses in detail its reasons for not accepting certain recommendations made in comment letters and hearings. This time, however, it did not even mention the existence of comments of the type quoted above, let alone address the criticisms.

Users do not like these nonprofit financial statements. Bond-rating agencies require nonprofit organizations to submit special reports in which current transactions are separated from contributed capital transactions. The Internal Revenue Service, in an unusual move, permits nonprofit organizations to depart from FASB rules when completing Form 990, its annual required report; that type of permission is unusual. The U.S. Department of Education permits colleges and universities to disregard the FASB rules in preparing its required annual report, "Integrated Post Secondary Education Data System."

Many nonprofit organizations do not use the financial information required by the new rules. Instead, they prepare the prescribed Statement of Unrestricted Activities (the FASB's name for a nonprofit Income Statement), and within that statement they embed a report of operating performance. Because organizations have different definitions of "operating," their financial statements are not comparable.

Defects

The case for a complete set of standards for nonprofit organizations is not strong. Even if there were such a set, it should not be organized into the three classes described in CON 6.

Operating Statement

All organizations need a report of performance, that is, a report of revenues (including gains) and expenses (including losses). In a business enterprise this report is the Income Statement. A similar statement is needed in a nonprofit organization. Were it not for tradition, the bottom line on such a statement would be labeled "Net Income"; it would be defined in the same way as the bottom line on a business Income Statement. The transactions that affect contributed capital should be excluded from the measurement of Net Income.

In short, neither the FASB nor the AICPA has described the measurement of Net Income or its equivalent in nonprofit organizations.

Example: Ivy League.[4] Exhibit 6 gives 1996 numbers for the eight Ivy League schools: Brown, Columbia, Cornell, Dartmouth, Harvard, the University of Pennsylvania, Princeton, and Yale. These are a tiny fraction of the 3,000 colleges and universities in the United States, and the higher education industry is only one of many nonprofit industries. Although the sample size is small, the endowments of these universities are large, and so the exhibit dramatically illustrates the unsatisfactory nature of the new rules for nonprofit organizations in general.

The "Unrestricted Surplus" column in the exhibit gives the excess of revenues over expenses, calculated according to the new rules; they are the "bottom line." Four of the eight schools reported an unrestricted surplus of $300 million or more, and six reported amounts that were 15 percent or more of revenue. These numbers obviously do not measure actual performance. The most grotesque number is Yale's. Yale had financial difficulties in 1996; it certainly did not generate a surplus of $536 million, which was 58 percent of revenue.

Considering that a Net Income of 10 or 15 percent of revenue is quite good for a profit-oriented business, these percentages are ridiculous for nonprofit organizations. If these

Exhibit 6
Ivy League Operating Performance Measures
FY 1996 ($ thousands)

	Unrestricted Revenue	Unrestricted Surplus	% Revenue	Operating Surplus Reported	Operating Surplus Adjusted
Brown	$ 331,174	$ 18,695	6	$ 7,831	$ 7,831
Columbia	1,275,216	314,447	25	69,947	3,916
Cornell	1,637,575	299,730	18	12,090	(19,370)
Dartmouth	336,493	51,848	15	120	1,121
Harvard	1,518,711	460,257	30	(2,274)	42,260
Penn	1,946,198	124,900	6	43,749	43,749
Princeton	602,458	538,998	89	223	15,234
Yale	920,877	536,432	58	(7,469)	(7,469)

schools actually had the huge surpluses that were reported, parents would question the amount of tuition they paid, faculty members would conclude that their schools could afford to pay higher salaries, and donors would question the need for their contributions.

A distortion arises because, as was mentioned above, the FASB has specified that all contributions that are not legally restricted by the donor are unrestricted revenues. The Ivy League statements reported contributions of huge amounts that had nothing to do with 1996 operations. Some reported additions to endowments were contributions that were not specified as such by the donors. In many schools these board-designated endowments constitute about a fourth of the total endowment; they are not available to finance operating activities except in an extreme financial emergency. Similarly, 2001 contributions of buildings and equipment do not provide funds to pay 2001 bills.

Similarly, part of the gains in the market value of endowment securities should be added to the endowment principal to preserve the endowment's purchasing power; they are not revenues in the current year. Few, if any, expenses are associated with these items, and so including them as revenue results in almost an equal increase in the bottom line.

The receipt of nonoperating items included in the "Unrestricted Revenue" column is erratic. Amounts of "revenue" from a capital campaign, gains and losses on endowment funds, bequests for board-designated endowments, and contributed buildings and equipment vary greatly among organizations and from one year to the next. They therefore distort comparisons with other schools and with amounts in prior years. Because no expenses typically are associated with these revenue items, their effect on unrestricted surplus is also erratic. Ironically, while many FASB pronouncements in the for-profit sector are designed to *smooth* earnings, these pronouncements have had the opposite effect in the nonprofit sector.

The financial officers in the Ivy League schools knew that the numbers for unrestricted revenue and unrestricted surplus calculated according to the new rules were misleading. Moreover, ratios of individual expense amounts, using revenue as 100 percent, are also useless. As a result, not one financial officer mentioned these numbers in the explanations accompanying a financial statement or in press releases.

The Ivy League schools reported an operating surplus number as shown in the "Reported Operating Surplus" column in Exhibit 6. The FASB rules give no guidance as to how that number should be calculated. Lacking such guidance, the schools developed their own rules.

Those rules differed in regard to the treatment of new plant. Dartmouth and Yale included a revenue item for plant assets placed in service. Almost all of Columbia's reported operating surplus was due to a $62.6 million "increase in plant net assets available for construction."

In the last column of Exhibit 6 I adjusted the numbers to estimate what the operating surplus would have been if the schools had excluded nonoperating contributions and otherwise had used generally accepted accounting principles (GAAP). I excluded the amount for "plant placed in service" from revenue; new plant certainly is not current-year revenue in any sensible meaning of that word. I did not attempt to adjust for the accounting of gains and losses; the new rules for treating these items are extraordinarily complicated, and I could not determine how they were applied.

Obviously, the schools did not use consistent rules. As is shown in the last two columns, the operating surpluses reported by Columbia and Cornell are higher than their actual operating surpluses; the numbers for Dartmouth, Harvard, and Princeton are lower.

There are indications that some schools transferred their operating surplus to nonoperating accounts, which is not permitted under FASB rules. Dartmouth's reported surplus of $120,000 is 0.0004 percent of its revenue (i.e., essentially breakeven). While Dartmouth *could* have obtained this unusual result by luck in one year, it reported that it had obtained a similar result for six consecutive years. That is neither luck nor good accounting; it is simply the use of an arbitrary accounting transfer to adjust the bottom line to almost zero.

Probably there are other differences that I did not detect.

All the Ivy League financial statements received a clean opinion from either Deloitte & Touche or Coopers & Lybrand. Coopers & Lybrand called attention to Harvard's treatment of depreciation in its opinion letter, but there were no comments in the other letters. All the opinion letters said, "In our opinion, the 1996 financial statements present fairly in all material respects the [financial statements listed] in conformity with generally accepted accounting principles." Readers who note the differences described above no doubt will ask, How can they all be in conformity with GAAP?

Bottom Line

In most organizations that have significant amounts of endowment the FASB rules require that all earnings on that endowment, including unrealized gains on the stock market portfolio, be reported as unrestricited revenue. In years of high market appreciation this clearly results in an overstatement of revenues compared with what actually was available for operating purposes, resulting in an unrealistically high bottom line. Most users of financial statements expect a nonprofit organization to spend almost all its operating revenues and therefore have a bottom line that is close to zero. They are seriously misled by bottom lines that reflect the FASB's rules.

Advance Payments

As was noted above, the FASB staff invented the temporarily restricted class as a solution to what it thought was a problem relating to one type of contribution: advance payments for projects to be conducted in a future year or for some other future purpose. In business accounting and often in nonprofit practice, advance payments are treated as liabilities in the year in which they are received; they could easily reflect this fact without the use of a separate fund classification.[5]

Pledges

Most pledges of contributed capital with payment promised in one or more future years are made in response to a capital fund drive. Before Financial Accounting Standard (FAS) 116 organizations either did not report those pledges in the financial statements or reported them in a note rather than on the balance sheet.

FAS116 (¶ 115) requires that "legally enforceable" pledges be reported as temporarily restricted assets at their present value in the year in which they are received. Because the formula for present value automatically results in annual increases, the amount of a pledge also increases each year. For example, a pledge of payment to be made five years hence would be recorded at approximately 75 percent of the pledged amount in the year received, and that amount would increase each year thereafter until 100 percent was paid. FAS116 requires that this annual increase be reported as contribution revenue.

Reporting a pledge payable in a future year as revenue in the current year is a peculiar way of earning revenue. Such a pledge is similar to a sales order. A promise of payment to be made in future years for amounts expended in those years is not revenue in the current year.

Moreover, requiring that only legally enforceable pledges be reported results in the worst possible situation. Apart from the question of what "legally enforceable" means in terms of a pledge, if an organization decides to reports pledges, it should report *all* valid pledges, not only those which are legally enforceable. It then might use an allowance similar to a bad debt allowance to account for some portion of the pledges that would not be received.

Board-Designated Endowments

Unless a donor specifies that his or her addition to an endowment is restricted, the contribution must be reported as unrestricted revenue. Many contributions clearly are intended to be additions to endowment even though the donor does not specify that. Using carefully constructed rules for identifying contributions intended for endowment, the previous practice was to classify them as "board-designated" (also "quasi") endowment. Reporting them as operating revenue seriously distorts the report of operating performance, as was shown in the Ivy League example.

Gains and Losses on Endowment

An organization realizes a gain when it sells an asset for more than its cost. Many organizations add endowment gains to the endowment principal; the trust laws of some states require this. Some organizations use the spending-rate method of recognizing endowment revenue. They recognize a specified percentage of the endowment's fair value as revenue. This number in effect includes interest, dividends, and a portion of endowment gains. Unless the donor specifies otherwise, the new FASB rules require that all realized gains be counted as unrestricted revenues. Similarly, realized losses are counted as expenses. The FASB requirement is contrary to sound, long-established practice. In some states it is contrary to law.

FAS124 (¶ 17) requires that the endowment portfolio be reported at fair value if fair values are available. Donors usually do not specify how the difference between cost and fair value should be treated. Under the new rules the difference must be recognized as unrestricted revenue or expense in the current period.

Depreciable Assets

FAS116 (¶ 16) permits either of two methods of reporting contributed capital assets and the related depreciation.

In one method the total cost of a contributed asset is reported as unrestricted revenue in the year in which the asset is placed in service. Clearly, this amount is not revenue earned in that year. Moreover, this asset amount is depreciated in future years; the depreciation charge is an expense that decreases the bottom line.

In the other method the contributed asset is reported as an addition to the temporarily restricted class when it is acquired. Depreciation expense is reported for each year thereafter, and the amount of depreciation expense is offset by an equal amount of unrestricted revenue (reported as a "reclassification"). Therefore, there is no effect on the bottom line; this is correct.

The simpler practice is not to recognize depreciation on

contributed depreciable assets. The bottom-line effect is the same as it is in the second method. Depreciation of a contributed asset is not an expense. Depreciation expense recovers the cost of an asset, and the cost of a contributed asset is zero. Depreciation expense is not intended to provide for the replacement of an asset, as some people assert. Depreciation provides for the original cost of an asset, and the same amount cannot be thought of as also providing for its replacement.

The rules for an item as important as depreciation should not permit an organization to select from one of two alternatives that have significantly different impacts on the bottom line.

Expenses

FAS117 (¶ 20) requires that all expenses be reported as decreases in unrestricted net assets and hence in the bottom line. As used in FAS117, "expenses" include expenditures for capital campaigns. These are costs of the capital campaign and properly are netted against the proceeds of the campaign; they are not expenses as this term usually is defined. Expenses in FAS117 should include costs associated with the operating assets owned by the endowment funds (e.g., the operation of a hotel, store, or apartment house). These expenditures properly are charged to the endowment. They have nothing to do with a nonprofit organization's operating activities.

Single Balance Sheet

Until FAS117 was implemented, most nonprofit organizations had at least two balance sheets (or two separate sections in a single balance sheet): one for assets and liabilities related to the organization's own activities and the other for contributed capital assets and liabilities. This separation reflects the fact that the management of an organization's own activities is entirely separate from the management of endowment and other contributed capital. The underlying reason is similar to the reason for not mixing pension fund assets and liabilities with other assets and liabilities on a business balance sheet.

FAS117 requires a single balance sheet, that is, a balance sheet that does not separate an organization's own assets and liabilities from endowment assets and liabilities. Many nonprofit organizations invest endowment funds in partnerships, retail stores, apartment houses, hotels, or other entities that have assets and liabilities. Mixing the assets and liabilities of those investments with operating assets and liabilities hides the numbers for an organization's own activities. Analysts need the numbers for an organization's own activities to study that organization's financial status. Cash held in the plant fund temporarily to pay bills for construction costs is not available to pay suppliers and employees.

Ratios and other comparisons that analysts make of balance sheet items have meaning only if an organization's own activities are separated from nonoperating assets and liabilities.

Reporting Fund Status

Footnote 5 of FAS117 maintains, "This Statement does not preclude providing disaggregated information by fund groups." Fund groups do not have a one-to-one correspondence with the three classes of equity, making it impossible to prepare a statement in which individual funds are listed under one of the three classes. For example, the endowment fund contains (1) the amount of board-designated endowment, which is in the unrestricted class, (2) the amount of term endowment, which is in the temporarily restricted class, and (3) the amount of donor-designated endowment, which is in the permanently restricted class. The assets of these separate types of endowment are pooled for investment purposes. (There may be two pools: one for term endowment and

the other for permanent endowment.) The amount of endowment earnings recognized under the spending-rate method is
calculated from the sum of those assets. Dividing them
among the separate classes is artificial and obscures the status
of endowment as a whole.

Statement of Cash Flows

FAS117 requires a nonprofit Statement of Cash Flows that is
similar to a business Statement of Cash Flows. (Note that
FAS95, on the Statement of Cash Flows, uses the term "operations," but the drafters of FAS117 said that they could not define this term.) The nonprofit Statement of Cash Flows mixes
together flows in all three classes of equity. For this reason, the
Statement of Cash Flows required by FAS117 is not useful.

On the typical Cash Flow Statement of an organization with
significant amounts of endowment, the two largest items are
the purchases of securities and proceeds from the sales of securities. For example, in 2000 Harvard reported $52.1 *billion* of
purchases and $56.6 *billion* of sales. These items, although
huge, are of trivial importance for analysis. At most, they
identify possible churning. Businesses, by contrast, are not required to provide such information.

No Evidence of Usefulness

Presumably, the principal reason for requiring the three
classes is the belief that the new model will provide more useful information than the old model did. If the information is
indeed more useful, its uses generally will be described in the
literature. There has been no outpouring of literature or evidence of acceptance in practice in response to this requirement. There are articles, conferences, meetings, and work-
shops on how to cope with the complicated accounting, but
they are designed for accountants, not for users.[6]

The FASB claims that the new standards increase consistency, and indeed, the standards are the same for all nonprofit organizations. However, if the standards are not useful, the fact that they are consistent is not relevant. Consistent garbage is still garbage.

The only tribute to the standards' usefulness that I am aware of is Robert H. Northcutt's article in the June 1995 *Accounting Horizons*. Northcutt was an FASB board member, and he alleged that public reaction to the new standards "has been extremely favorable." I asked him for the evidence supporting that statement, and he responded with one favorable article by FASB personnel and by quoting excerpts from only one (yes, *only one*) letter to the FASB and nine articles. He asked me to publish those quotations, and I did so in the September 1995 issue of *Accounting Horizons*.

Not one of the 10 quotations comes from a board member or an executive in a nonprofit organization. Only one is from a letter to the FASB, and that quotation is part of one sentence. The other nine are excerpts from publications ranging in length from part of one sentence to two paragraphs. Seven of these quotations were from little-known trade papers (e.g., *Atlanta Business Chronicle, Denver Business Journal*). Not one describes a specific use of the new information; all are vague generalities, and some contain out-and-out errors.

The examples from the negative quotes are: "Accounting changes pose a serious threat to college,"[7] "Colleges are dealt a blow,"[8] and "Not-for-profits wince at effect of FASB statements."[9]

U.S. Department of Education. The U.S. Department of Education installed a new system for measuring the performance of colleges and universities. It attempted to adjust for the overstatement of revenue in the new rule, but the result was a hodgepodge of numbers that had no valid reasoning.

Rating Agencies. Moody's published a list of nonprofit ratios in its house publication, *Perspectives*, on August 16, 1996. Those ratios did not use any of the totals of the three classes of equity or changes in those classes. Moody's adjusts the change in unrestricted equity to arrive at what it thinks is a proxy for changes in unrestricted equity, and it makes a similar adjustment for the total of permanently restricted equity. It makes no use whatsoever of the temporarily restricted class.

Paucity of Criticism. The reader may ask, If the FASB system is as poor as I have demonstrated, why has it not generated an uproar of disapproval? The attitude of many users is summarized in a letter from the treasurer of a large nonprofit organization:

> The transition to FAS116 and 117 has been so arduous that I doubt that any of my colleagues would willingly undertake another change in the foreseeable future.

Remedies

General

There is no need to require a unique accounting system for nonprofit organizations. The three categories listed in CON 6 and in FAS116 and 117—unrestricted, temporarily restricted, and permanently restricted—should be rescinded. A standard on contributed capital (i.e., plant, museum objects, and endowment) should be developed. Other transactions should be treated the same in nonprofit organizations as they are in businesses. This would reinstate practices formerly used by well-managed nonprofit organizations. There should be a separate statement of contributed capital. Contributed assets should be reported separately from operating assets because they are not available to finance operating activities; endowment cash cannot legally be used to pay the light bill.

There should be a statement that reports changes in contributed capital during the period. Increases and decreases in contributed capital are not revenues and expenses; revenues and expenses relate to operating activities.

Some of the FASB's nonprofit rules should be changed.

For example, the use of depreciation on contributed plant is not logically defensible. There are also problems in accounting for resource inflows that one nonprofit organization receives and passes on to another. In principle, these inflows are similar to the income tax withholding amounts that business organizations have. The use of endowment pools, especially in the treatment of gains and losses, should be described.

Revenues

As was pointed out above, several types of resource inflows that are included as unrestricted revenues are in fact contributed capital. Although many additions to endowment are not legally unrestricted, their large size or other characteristics make it clear that they were not intended to be used to finance the current year's activities. Organizations welcome these "board-designated" endowments because they can be included in debt coverage ratios, something that is not possible with legal endowment.

The FASB requires that investment gains of endowment funds be reported as unrestricted. Although the attorneys general of several states have ruled that in some circumstances they can be added to endowment, the current situation is murky. FAS124, "Accounting for Certain Investments Held by Not-for-Profit Organizations," spells out the rules. They are extraordinarily complicated; those complications would be unnecessary if additions to endowment (including gains) were treated in the methods used previously.

Although this is almost unbelievable, the rules state that one option for accounting for the cost of a contributed building is to book the amount as unrestricted revenue in the period in which it is placed in service. A $10 million building is not a $10 million source of operating revenue in the year in which it is placed in service.

Advance Payments

As was described above, some advance payments from contributors are classified as exchange transactions and reported as liabilities and others are classified as contributions and reported as additions to temporarily restricted equity. In some cases, part of the payment is an exchange transaction and part is a contribution.

The line between these two types of payments is vague. One of the 11 sections in the FASB continuing professional education volume on not-for-profit accounting is devoted to this topic. It consists of 14 pages of text and diagrams. The *AICPA Not-for-Profit Accounting Guide* has five pages on how to make such a separation. The simple alternative is to report all these payments as liabilities.

Depreciation

FAS93 requires that long-lived assets owned by an entity be depreciated. (This is an alternative to the treatment of newly acquired assets mentioned above.) These assets had zero cost to the entity, and so there was no cost to be recovered. Subsequent to the issuance of FAS93, on depreciation, the FASB seems to have recognized this logical inconsistency, and FAS116 states that this depreciation must be offset by an item of unrestricted revenue in an equal amount. Consequently, there is no effect on income but much extra bookkeeping.

Pledges

The FASB rules require that long-term pledges be reported in financial statements at the present value of a pledge. This amount is updated annually. Another of the 11 sections in the FASB continuing professional education volume deals primarily with this topic. A record of each pledge should of course be maintained, but the additional record keeping required for the present value calculation is of little use. Indeed, the "revenue" resulting from this calculation is misleading. Pledges for the current year should be booked as a receivable. Pledges for a capital purpose should be reported in a note, which was the previous practice.

Endowment Gains and Losses

The treatment of realized gains and losses on endowment is governed by the donor's specific statement about whether the contribution is restricted. The simpler solution is to assign all realized gains and losses to each endowment fund, including board-designated endowment, in proportion to the principal of each one unless there are specific reasons to do otherwise. Some organizations have hundreds, and a few have thousands, of separate endowment funds. The task of complying with the FASB requirement is onerous. These rules require that as many as seven separate decisions be made for each endowment in order to assign gains and losses to the proper class.[10]

Contributions Made

FAS116 and 117 describe the accounting required by contributors as well as that required by the recipient nonprofit organizations. Actually, contributors account for contributions just as they do for other expenditures. The new rules require a different treatment for pledges and certain advance payments, but these requirements make no sense and should be deleted.

Contributed Personal Services

FAS116 (¶ 9) states, "Personal services shall be recognized if the services received (a) create or enhance nonfinancial assets or (b) require specialized skills provided by individuals possessing those skills and would typically need to be purchased." A conceptual argument can be made to justify this requirement, but as a practical matter it poses many problems. For example, lawyers who are board members may help with legal matters, but they probably do not expect this help to be recognized formally.

In September 1987 the FASB surveyed 5,500 preparers of not-for-profit financial reports, targeting larger organizations in an effort to capture a representative group of the types of not-for-profit organizations. When asked their opinions about publicly disclosing the dollar amount for contributed services, only 17 percent agreed there should be such disclosure. A significant number of preparers and users of not-for-profit financial reports agreed that recognizing contributed services by imputing a dollar value is not useful.

Nonreciprocal Transfers

The FASB relies on the concept of nonreciprocal transfer, which is defined as a transaction in which the entity receives cash or other assets from an outside party but does not give goods or services in return. This concept is described in APB Opinion No. 29, adopted in 1973 and emphasized as recently as 1999. In an FASB special report[11] such a transfer is said to be distinguished from an "exchange transaction." This is a distinction without a difference. A contribution for current purposes is revenue just as much as are resource inflows from a sale. This minor matter is mentioned because the FASB sometimes uses it as a justification for its treatment of contributions.

Cash Flow Statement

A Statement of Cash Flows is necessary for operating activities for the same reasons it is useful in business. I doubt that cash flow information is useful for contributed capital flows because cash flows are almost the same as increases and decreases in contributed capital items; those increases and decreases should be reported.

Terminology

The special terms that the FASB uses for accounting in nonprofit organizations—"Statement of Activities," "Net Assets," "Change in Net Assets," "Statement of Changes in Net Assets," "conditional promise to give," "unrestricted support"— should be replaced by the terms used in business financial statements. These differences in terminology imply that there are more differences in substance between business and nonprofit accounting than actually exist.

Notes

[1] Audits of Colleges and Universities (1973); Audits of Voluntary Health and Welfare Organizations (1974); SOP 78–10, "Accounting Principles and Reporting Practices of Certain Non-Profit Organizations" (1978); Audits of Providers of Health Care Services.

[2] One reviewer said that the material was "sour grapes" because I had written the report that was disregarded. Actually, FASB staff members had commented on my material, but no one raised questions about the accuracy of the facts I listed.

[3] This sentence was added to the exposure draft in an attempt to meet the widespread request for a distinction between operating capital and contributed capital. It does not meet their requests, but to do so would have required an amendment to CON 6, and the FASB had never amended a concepts statement.

[4] This section is adapted from my article "Apples and Oranges at Your Alma Mater," *The Wall Street Journal*, November 14, 1997.

[5] The Financial Accounting Foundation receives advance payments from subscribers. The obvious treatment here is to treat them as liabilities when they are received and as revenue when the items are published, just as is the case with newspaper and magazine subscriptions. Some argue that an advance payment for costs on a conference or a research project is not a liability because the nonprofit organization may not legally be required to return the money if the project is not held or the project is not undertaken. This is a specious argument. The organization has a moral obligation to return the funds, and its reputation would be harmed if it did not do so.

[6] The few articles that purport to describe useful information from the new

financial statements describe numbers that are not in fact available for organizations that have endowment or plant. See, for example, KPMG Peat Marwick and Prager McCarthy & Sealy, *Ratio Analysis in Higher Education: Measuring Past Performance to Chart Future Direction*, KPMG Peat Marwick, Chicago, 1995.

[7] An article titled "Accounting Changes Pose a Serious Threat to Colleges" by Peter Buchanan in *Chronicle of Higher Education*, April 21, 1991.

[8] An article titled "Colleges Are Dealt a Blow" by Liz McMillin in *Chronicle of Higher Education*, November 29, 1991.

[9] "Not-for-Profits Whine at Effect of FASB Statements," *Accounting Today*, July 25, 1994.

[10] For an excellent description of how difficult it is to apply these rules, see David T. Meeting, Randall W. Luecke, and Edward J. Giniat, "Understanding and Implementing FAS124," *Journal of Accountancy*, March 1996.

[11] Mark Westwood and April Mackenzie for the G4 + 1 organization. FASB *Financial Accounting Series*, "Accounting by Recipients for Non-Reciprocal Transfers, Excluding Contributions by Owners." This 65-page report assumes that there is something special about nonreciprocal transfers.

8

STATE AND LOCAL GOVERNMENT ACCOUNTING

Statement 34 of the Governmental Accounting Standards Board (GASB) requires two complete sets of financial statements: one called "government-wide accounting" and the other called "fund accounting." The fund-accounting financial statements are unnecessary and cause confusion. They should be eliminated.

Background

Beginning in the early twentieth century, most state and local government organizations used fund accounting to control spending. An organization had one bank account or "fund" for its payroll, another for supplies, another for travel costs, and others for each disbursement purpose. When the balance in an account dropped to zero, spending automatically stopped. However, managers and their accountants could beat the system by switching cash from one fund to another and incurring liabilities, which eventually had to be paid in cash.

151

Later the practice of having separate bank accounts for each fund was superseded by a system that accounted for funds within the system itself. Each fund contained asset, liability, and equity accounts, and those funds conformed to the basic equation Assets = Liabilities + Equity. A government could have dozens or even hundreds of those funds.

Standards for government accounting were set by the National Council on Governmental Accounting (NCGA), an organization financed by government bodies and accounting firms. Those standards were based on the fund-accounting principle.

Statement 34 of the GASB (1999), which required government organizations to use *both* the government-wide system and the fund-accounting system, was amended by Statements 35, 36, 37, and 38. Those changes do not affect the comments I will make in the next section.

Governmental Accounting Standards Board

In 1979 the Financial Accounting Foundation (FAF) accepted responsibility for establishing state and local government accounting standards. Initially, the FAF wanted those standards to be the responsibility of the existing Financial Accounting Standards Board (FASB). However, government organizations objected to that arrangement on the grounds that government accounting was essentially different from business accounting. They threatened to continue to rely on the NCGA and not to help the FAF financially or recognize its standards. As a compromise, the GASB was established in 1982; it reported to the FAF.

The initial board was impressive. One of its five members was the recently retired Comptroller General of the United States, and another was the managing partner of one of the leading U.S. accounting firms. The GASB's first pronouncement was made in 1984. It accepted the NCGA standards as authoritative until its own standards were developed.

In 1987 the GASB issued a concepts statement. Although that statement recognized the prevalence of fund accounting, it had a section on interperiod equity, a concept that is inconsistent with the fund approach. The interperiod equity idea was discussed at length in a December 1996 *Accounting Horizons* article titled "The Behavior of Interperiod Equity-Related Performance Measures Over Time" by Barry R. Marks and K. K. Raman (the interperiod equity concept is explained below). In its early years the GASB issued standards on specific topics but did not issue an overall standard.

The GASB could not agree on standards to implement the concepts statement. Some members favored fund accounting, while others favored a businesslike approach.

Statement 11

In 1990 the GASB issued Statement 11. That statement required an accrual system similar to systems used by businesses and conforming to rules of the FASB, the International Accounting Standards Board (IASB), and the standards-setting organizations in many countries. The GASB called that system "government-wide accounting."

The foundation of the system was the interperiod equity concept. This concept states that financial performance in a given year is satisfactory if the taxes paid, or likely to be paid, by the taxpayers for that year at least equal the costs of the services provided to them that were not financed by other sources. If citizens pay lower taxes than this, they shift a financial burden to taxpayers in future years. If taxes are higher than the breakeven amount, the taxpayers are paying more than is needed to finance the year's activities. (The excess may be deliberate to provide a safety factor.)

In accounting terms, this concept means that financial performance in a given year is equitable if revenues at least equal expenses. Revenues and expenses in this case have the same meaning that they have in private-sector accounting. Revenues include resources available for operating purposes but do not include grants for acquiring plant or other resource inflows that are not available to finance the current year's expenses. Expenses include the cost of resources used during the period, as in business accounting.

Many government accountants disliked this system, which was drastically different from the fund-accounting system they had used for many years. To allow time to resolve the differences between them and those who favored a business-like approach, Statement 11 did not have an implementation date.

Statement 34

Some of the original GASB members ended their terms in 1994. Their successors were accountants who were accustomed to the fund-accounting system; one, in fact, had been the principal author of the NCGA standards. In Statement 34, "Basic Financial Statements—and Management's Discussion and Analysis—for State and Local Governments," issued in 1999 the board required government organizations to use *both* systems: government-wide accounting and fund accounting.

The board cited "accountability" as its justification for continuing to use the fund-accounting system. Some of the resources available to an organization specified the purposes for which those resources could be used. Each category of resources that was limited in that manner was recorded in a separate fund, and the organization was *accountable* for spending those resources for the specified purpose.

Revenues and Expenses

Transactions that are revenues and expenses in the government-wide system are listed below.

Revenues (including gains)[1] are inflows of current resources, that is, resources that are available to pay for current-year expenses. They include the following:[2]

- Taxes applicable to the year
- Grants and other outside sources of funds used to finance work done during the year
- Revenues earned for goods and services provided to outside parties during the year
- Endowment earnings applicable to the year
- Gains on the sale of operating assets during the year
- Net income of business-type activities for the year
- Extraordinary and unusual resource inflows associated with operating activities

In general, contributions and taxes are revenues unless they clearly are not intended for use in the current year. This intention may be stated specifically or may be implied. For example, the contribution of a building obviously does not provide cash that can be used to pay for expenses in the current year.

Revenues do not include resource inflows that will be used for operating activities in future years. Those inflows create a liability. They do not include additions to endowment and similar inflows that are not available to finance the current year's expenses.

Expenses, including losses, are outflows of resources for activities of the current year. They include the following:[3]

- Compensation for the services of employees during the year for which they were or will be paid, including pensions and other benefits to which employees are entitled even though the payments will be made in future years
- Cost of materials used during the year
- Cost of services provided by organizations outside the government entity
- Depreciation of assets acquired with operating resources
- Losses on the sale of assets acquired with operating resources
- Net loss of business-type activities for the year

Expenses do not include the costs incurred in managing the endowment or depreciation on contributed capital assets.

International Federation of Accountants

Beginning in 2000, the International Federation of Accountants issued a set of standards entitled "International Public Sector Accounting Standards" that were applicable to all federal, state, and local governments. These standards are not likely to be adopted generally. The International Federation of Accountants has no enforcement power, and the standards mostly are adapted from those of the IASB, but with no recognition of the special accounting rules that should be used for government organizations. I therefore do not discuss them further.

Defects

Unnecessary Accountability Information

Statement 34, paragraph 2, defines accountability as follows:

> Accountability is the paramount objective of governmental financial reporting—the objective from which all other financial reporting objectives flow. Government's duty to be accountable includes providing financial information that is useful for economic, social, and political decisions. Financial reports that contribute to these decisions include information useful for (a) comparing actual financial results with the legally adopted budget, (b) assessing the financial condition and results of operations, (c) assisting in determining compliance with finance-related laws, rules, and regulations, and (d) assisting in evaluating efficiency and effectiveness.

The following four paragraphs show the fund-accounting section of Statement 34 requires more information than is necessary to meet the accountability objective:

"Comparing actual financial results with the legally adopted budget." A "legally adopted budget" is one that is voted in by a state legislative body, an elected city council, or a similar body or is voted in directly by citizens. The government must, of course, comply with it. If this budget is prepared on the traditional fund-accounting basis, the government-wide system will not provide the information needed to assure compliance. Fund accounts therefore must be created to match this budget. However, there is no need to include this information in the general-purpose financial statements. If there is compliance with this requirement, no notice of this fact is necessary. If there is noncompliance, the auditor must call attention to that fact. Presumably, the body that insists on compliance with such a budget will soon see that this extra record keeping is unnecessary. It will then shift to a budget prepared on the government-wide basis.

"Assessing the financial condition and results of operations." This objective is accomplished with the government-wide financial statements.

"Assisting in determining compliance with finance-related laws, rules, and regulations." As was mentioned above, the auditor is required to call attention to any material noncompliance. Additional detail is not necessary.

"Assisting in evaluating efficiency and effectiveness." Compliance with this objective requires information about outcomes that most organizations do not have. Both government accounting and business accounting are unable to provide much information, although the GASB is developing many possibilities.[4] Statement 34 does not attempt to provide data that help accomplish this objective.

Statement 34 requires that information on 11 funds be reported. In eight of those funds the government-wide system contains the same information as the fund-accounting system except that some government-wide accounts do not identify specific assets assigned to the fund. A ninth fund, the internal service fund, is useful only for management purposes; it does not belong in a general-purpose financial statement prepared for outside parties. The remaining two funds provide confusing information, as is described below.

Accounting for funds differs from accounting in the government-wide system in two principal respects.

First, the fund-accounting system identifies assets that are available to meet the liabilities and purposes of each fund. By contrast, the government-wide system focuses on assets and liabilities as a whole without attempting to assign assets to specific funds unless there is a valid reason to do so, such as a donor's requirement that the fund be invested in specified assets. The asset amount reported for a fund is simply the book-keeping amount required to make total debits equal total credits. Again, the auditor must call attention to any noncompliance. The fund-accounting statement does not call attention to noncompliance in any individual fund; it reports totals for each *type* of fund.

Second, the fund-accounting system is limited to short-term (almost "current") liabilities, whereas the government-wide system includes *all* liabilities.

The following descriptions are essential to understanding the nature of the fund accounts.

Capital project funds account for the cost of constructing or acquiring major capital assets. These amounts are reported as an asset labeled "construction in progress" in the government-wide balance sheet. Managers who are responsible for overseeing a capital project need information about the amounts spent and any limits on construction costs, but this is management accounting information and makes only a small contribution if any, to reporting on accountability.[5]

Debt service funds account for principal and interest payments on bonded debt. In the government-wide system, principal payments are debits to liability and interest payments are expenses (unless they are capitalized as an item of construction cost). Debt service information is useful for financial planning purposes, but this level of detail does not have to be included in general-purpose financial statements. "Sinking funds" are a special type of debt service fund. If the amount and type of assets that can be used only to make payments on outstanding bonds are specified in the bond indenture, those amounts are recorded in a sinking fund that is separated from other assets. Sinking funds are reported in the government-wide accounts.

Permanent funds (also called endowment) report resources that are legally restricted to the extent that only earnings—not principal—may be used for purposes that support the government's programs. They are reported as such in the government-wide accounts.

Agency funds are used to report resources held by the reporting government in a purely custodial capacity; the asset amount is equal to the liability amount. Examples are taxes collected by one government on behalf of another government (such as payroll withholding taxes) and taxes for local schools collected by a county. Receipts from deferred-compensation plans are accounted for in agency funds. Also, amounts received from special assessments made for work the government will do for another party, such as building roads and sidewalks in a housing project, are recorded in an agency fund.

If the assets in an agency fund must be segregated from other assets, the government-wide system accounts for them in a way similar to the one used in the fund system. At the initiation of the fund there is a record of the assets and an equal liability to the outside party. As the assets are used for the stated purpose, the balance decreases and there is an equal decrease in the liability. This is what happens in fund accounting. The same entries are made in the government-wide system regardless of whether the word "fund" is used.

Pension funds and other employee benefit funds are used "to report resources that are required to be held in trust for the members and beneficiaries of defined benefit pension plans, defined contribution plans, other postemployment benefit plans, or other employee benefit plans" (paragraph 70). The debits and credits are the same in both government-wide accounting and fund accounting except that the amounts in fund accounting may be based on expenditures rather than expenses.

If the funds are managed by a state-sponsored agency, the local government does not oversee those assets and there are no entries in either a government-wide account or fund account once the payments have been made to the outside agency.

Investment trust funds are "used to report the external portion of investment pools reported by the sponsoring government" (paragraph 71). The amounts are the same in both accounting systems.

Private-purpose trust funds are "used to report all other trust arrangements under which principal and income benefit individuals, private organizations, or other governments" (paragraph 72). The amounts are the same in the government-wide and fund systems.

Enterprise funds account for activities for which a fee is charged to external users. An electric utility is an example of such an activity. The numbers used in enterprise funds in fund accounting are essentially the same as those used for "business-type activities" in government-wide accounting. In both reports inflows of resources are measured by revenues, and outflows by expenses. The bottom line is the same number. The differences are solely ones of nomenclature—"enterprise" in one case, "business-type" in the other—and different labels for some of the individual items. The traditional labels may be helpful to current preparers and users, but new preparers and users can learn the details of both sets of labels easily. Therefore, there is no need for two reports on enterprise funds: one in the government-wide statements and the other in the fund statements.

Internal service funds report on activities that provide goods or services to other departments or agencies. A motor pool is an example. The statement of activities in the fund-accounting system reports the charges made by those funds as costs of the unit that receives the goods or services. If the service activity operates at a deficit in a given period, the deficit is a cost of that period. In the government-wide system the charges are expenses rather than expenditures. Users of general-purpose financial statements do not need this information; it is simply an accounting device.

The financial performance and status of an organization and activities are reported in the *general fund* and *special revenue funds*. Although it is not defined, the general fund reports most of those activities. Special revenue funds account for taxes and other resource inflows that are earmarked for a designated purpose.

In summary, almost all the useful information provided by the fund-accounting system can be obtained from the government-wide system.

Different Numbers

Another defect of Statement 34 is that the two separate sets of required financial statements result in different numbers for the same item. In the government-wide system outflows of resources are measured as expenses, but in the fund-accounting system they are measured as expenditures.

Consider these examples of outflows taken from the sample financial statements in Statement 34:

	($000 omitted)	
	Government-wide Expense	Funds Expenditure
General government	$ 9,571	$ 8,631
Public safety	34,854	33,730
Public works	10,129	4,976
Health and sanitation	6,739	6,070
Culture and recreation	11,532	11,412

The examples are similar, but they are not identical. The differences are likely to raise the questions, Why have two numbers? and Which is better?

There also are differences in the measurement of revenues. Property taxes in fund accounting are measured as revenue when they are "available," which means during the period for which they are levied or shortly thereafter. Property taxes in the government-wide system are measured as the taxes due for the period, less an allowance for unpaid taxes. In the illustration, the fund-accounting property tax was $55,853,628 (Exhibit C-2 of Statement 34) and the government-wide property tax was $56,419,817 (Exhibit B-1). The discrepancy is not large, but it is enough to make the reader question why they are two different numbers with the same label for the same period and to wonder which one is better. (Of course, the amounts in sample exhibits give no indication of what the magnitude would be in practice.)

Balance sheet information is even more confusing. The government-wide balance sheet (Exhibit A-1, "Statement of Net Assets") reports cash and cash equivalents of $23.9 million. This is useful information. By contrast, the several fund balance sheets report $10.3 million of cash in government funds (Exhibit C-1), $8.7 million in business-type activities (Exhibit D-2), and $3.3 million in internal service funds (also Exhibit D-2) for a total of $22.3 million. The fund information is useless; the relevant amount is the organization's total cash. There is similar confusion in other balance sheet items. The more meaningful balance sheet is that for the government as a whole, divided into government and business-type activities, as is done in Exhibit A-1. Those numbers are consistent with the interperiod equity concept. The fund-accounting numbers are not consistent with this concept.

Worst of all is the "bottom line." The bottom lines on the various financial performance reports follow:

The "net cash from operating activities" (D-4) was $1,921,872
The "change in fund balance" (C-2, C-3)
  was a negative   (106,657)
Government-wide performance reports (B-1, B-2, B-4b)
  show a "change in net assets" of   105,599
"Change in budgetary fund balance" (G-1)
  was a negative   (1,310,546)

Thus, there are four measures of operating performance, each with a different label. They are reported on seven different required statements. Also, this tally omits several other statements in which detailed aspects of operating performance must be reported.

These different numbers for the same physical activities are confusing. They are reconciled in Exhibit C-3 and in a 14-page elaboration in notes 4a, 4b, 5a, and 5b. This reconciliation is not useful to a reader of financial statements. Presumably, users will use one set of numbers and disregard the other. They are unlikely to say, or think, "General government costs are either $9.6 million or $8.6 million, take your choice."

In general, the government-wide data conform to the generally accepted accounting principles (GAAP) used in business organizations and the fund-accounting reports use principles that were abandoned by most organizations, except the government, many years ago.

An alleged justification for continuing to use fund accounting is that its principles are closer than GAAP to the inflows and outflows of cash. This is so, but the numbers are not supposed to be inflows and outflows of cash. Accounting measures financial performance by the inflows and outflows of *resources*, not cash. When the FAF authorized the creation of the GASB, it surely did not expect the GASB to be bound by rules set by its predecessor. Furthermore, there is a cash flow report in the government-wide system.

The government-wide accounts will contain all the debits and credits for transactions that occur in the government entity because in the total system debits must equal credits. Some of these accounts are necessary to provide the information required by outside parties. Others simply report the entity's assets, liabilities, expenses, and revenues.

The implementation guide for Statement 34 seems to assume that both expenses and fund activities should be listed. This is a complicated task.

The government-wide focus measures expenses at the responsibility center that consumes resources, and fund accounting measures amounts incurred by the organization unit that makes the contract with an outside party; this amount is called an obligation. Thus, the two systems of accounting measure two different things in time and in place.

These differences do show up in the example given in Statement 34. Although the differences are not great, they may be significant in the real world.

I doubt that governments will in fact measure both government-wide and fund-accounting numbers because it would require too much work.

Unnecessary Details

The GASB system is more detailed than business systems.

Page 39 of Statement 34 is an example of the minutiae that government-wide accounting now requires. It discusses at length classifying activities, giving much more detail than do corresponding paragraphs in financial accounting standards.

GASB Statements 37 and 38 have several other examples of excessive detail.

An accounting standard should describe the format and content of general-purpose financial statements. Statement 34 does this, but it muddies the water by going too far. It describes a complete accounting system, including management accounting and bookkeeping procedures. Statement 34 has 400 pages, including about 100 pages of illustrations. This level of detail undoubtedly was intended to introduce government accountants to accrual accounting, but it asks too much. Governments may need to report somewhat more detail than do business, but certainly not the amount required by Statement 34.

Unnecessary Management Discussion

Statement 34 requires 20 items of "Management Discussion and Analysis." Business standards do not specify the details of such a discussion. In the sample the only reference to operating performance was that it was "virtually unchanged."

Contributed Capital Assets

Contributed capital assets are contributions that benefit future periods. They include contributions intended to be used to acquire capital assets (roads, bridges, buildings, equipment, museum objects) and contributions of funds whose earnings will be operating revenues in future periods (endowment), as well as grants made by another government or nongovernment agency and taxes levied to acquire capital assets. They do not include grants for projects; those grants are liabilities when received and become revenues when the project is worked on.

Capital contributions are similar to contributions made by the owners of a business. They add to equity but do not affect income in the period in which they were received.

Statements 33 and 34 count the receipt of all contributions as revenue in the period in which they were received. Statement 34 lists capital grants for specific programs as revenues of those programs. Grants that are not restricted to specific programs are revenues but are listed below operating expenses. If the contribution is a long-lived asset, Statement 34 requires reporting its acquisition at fair value and depreciating it over its estimated life.

Statement 34 does not define "revenue," but it does purport to rely on the interperiod equity concept defined in Concepts Statement 1. According to this concepts statement, revenues are resource inflows that pay for the services provided in the current year. It follows that a contribution benefiting several years, such as a three-year grant, is a liability when received and is revenue over each of the following years. A contribution of permanent capital, such as endowment, is never revenue; the earnings on that capital become revenue in the year in which they are earned. Counting a contributed capital contribution as revenue, whether it is reported above or below expenses, is wrong.

Moreover, the assets in which endowment funds are invested should be separated from other assets. Many states require this. Endowment cash cannot be used to pay operating bills. It is not a component of the current ratio or of a cash balance that may be required to be maintained. Statement 34 does not provide such a separation, and this also is wrong.

Depreciation

Reporting depreciation on contributed depreciable assets is inconsistent with the interperiod equity concept. In the current year, there is no resource outflow for depreciation of those assets, nor will there be an outflow in the future. The cost of the asset to the entity was zero, and the amount of current revenue required to pay for the asset is also zero. There will be a cost to replace the asset, but accounting does not record such a cost until the replacement takes place.

Long-lived assets acquired by contributions, including taxes levied specifically for that purpose, should not be depreciated.

For assets acquired with borrowed funds or operating surpluses, there is disagreement in the industry about whether depreciation should be based on historical cost or replacement cost. Australia and New Zealand are among the countries that are experimenting with replacement cost. I believe the interperiod equity concept requires that depreciation be based on historical cost.[6] Debt service on borrowed funds is an acceptable surrogate. Annuity depreciation is conceptually superior to straight-line depreciation, but it has few advocates.

Even if long-lived assets are not reported in the required financial statements, accurate records should be maintained, and those records should be reconciled with the accounting system. An entity should pay careful attention to the inventory of these assets. Some people argue that fixed assets have a cost and that the cost of operating an entity is understated unless depreciation of all assets is counted. This is so, but I know no convincing reason for using the actual cost of operating a government entity.

There is a precedent for the erroneous treatment of long-lived assets. In Financial Accounting Standard (FAS) 93, the FASB required that long-lived assets contributed to nonprofit organizations be recorded as assets and depreciated. However, in paragraph 16 of FAS116 the board corrected that error. That paragraph permits an amount equal to depreciation to be reported as revenue of the period; therefore, there is no effect on the bottom line. Of course, a simpler way of correcting this error would have been to delete the requirement that caused it.

The GASB fund-accounting system has no such error, and this is the only respect in which the fund-accounting system is better than the government-wide system. A nonexpendable trust fund (also called a permanent government fund) reports resources that are to be held in perpetuity or for a very long time. Only the earnings on those assets, not the principal, may be used to finance operations, and so only those earnings should be counted as revenue.

Contributed Capital

The principal difference between government accounting and business accounting is that government accounting has contributed capital. This is also the principal difference between nonprofit accounting and business accounting. In many nonprofit organizations the treatment of contributed capital was sound before FAS116 and 117.

Contributed capital should be accounted for separately from operating capital. There should be separate accounts for contributed plant (buildings, equipment, museum objects) and endowment. Additions to those accounts are not revenues, and reductions are not expenses. These changes are reported directly as increases or decreases in the contributed capital accounts. The cost of a capital campaign is a decrease in contributed capital.

Colleges and Universities

In the negotiations that led to the creation of the GASB, government people were successful in retaining jurisdiction for several industries that had both public and private members. One of those industries was higher education.[7]

A research report, an Invitation to Comment, an Exposure draft, and a standard were published over the next several years. They led to GASB Statement 35, which requires public colleges and universities to use Statement 34. Because some universities operate hospitals, Statement 35 also applies to hospital accounting. My previous comments about Statement 34 therefore apply also to college and university accounting.

Remedies

A Single System

The accounting system for state and local governments should be similar to the system for nonprofit organizations. (I explained the inadequacy of the current nonprofit system in Chapter 7.) Taxes and grants for operating purposes are the same as operating contributions in a nonprofit organization; both are revenues. Funds that will be used for capital purposes do require special accounting. This accounting is similar to that for contributions for plant and endowment in a nonprofit organization.

The 50 paragraphs on fund accounting in Statement 34 should be deleted for two reasons. First, as was pointed out above, information about funds is reported in the government-wide system. Repeating this information in a fund-accounting system is unnecessary. Compliance can be reported by stating whether the government complied with those requirements and, if not, what the noncompliance was. There is no need for any information about activities that did comply. Business financial statements do not even mention legal or contractual requirements unless the auditor discovers a violation.

Second, information reported in the general fund and the special revenue funds is less informative and more confusing than that reported in the government-wide system. The fact that these funds are less informative is demonstrated clearly in the GASB's own analysis. Under the heading "Operational Accountability," 21 paragraphs (214 through 234) of Statement 34 explain why a report of expenses, which is prepared in the government-wide system, is a better measure of performance than a system that reports only expenditures.

Requiring both a fund-accounting system and a government-wide system obviously requires more record keeping. Each fund is a self-balancing set of accounts that conforms to the equation Assets = Liabilities + Fund Balance. A "fund balance," as the name implies, balances the amounts in a fund. The government-wide system has no comparable item, but users can find the balance at any time by subtracting liabilities from assets.

Statement 34 is different from all other known standards. Instead of designating either expense or expenditure as the preferred way of reporting outflows, Statement 34 requires both. Most standards, including those of the FASB, the IASB, and British Commonwealth countries, require the use of expenses. The GASB requires the use of expenses for its government-wide focus *and* the use of expenditures for its funds focus. The actual cost of the resources used to provide services is the same in both settings. A standards-setting body should require only the principles it decides are the most useful.

A justification for continuing to collect information about the general fund and the special revenue funds is that if performance violates the legal requirements of those funds, noncompliance should be reported. This assumes the fund-accounting approach will continue to be required by the state or by another body that has the legal right to make such a requirement, a possibility that is highly unlikely. When a government begins to collect information in a government-wide system, there no longer will be a need for a general fund.

When the government-wide system is required for general-purpose financial statements, many governments will continue to use fund accounting for management purposes for several years, primarily because managers are familiar with it. As they become accustomed to accrual accounting, they will use fund accounting less often. Statement 34 in various places indicates that these funds help manage resources. Actually, the same information is available in the government-wide system. The revision of Statement 34 does not need to describe rules for fund accounting. For management control purposes, the organization can use whatever rules and format it wishes.

Omit Unnecessary Detail

Statement 34 requires much more detailed information than do other financial accounting standards. For example, in 1998 General Electric Company developed, manufactured, and marketed thousands of products that ranged from lightbulbs to television programs, operated in 100 countries, and had 293,000 employees, 2.1 million shareholders, and revenue of $100 billion. Its published balance sheet and income statement for that year have a total of 52 numbers. The corresponding government-wide statements for the much smaller sample cited in Statement 34 have 135 numbers—2.5 times as many. Much of this detail should be deleted. I do not describe the specific candidates for deletion because this would lead to pointless arguments over minutiae.

The FASB, the IASB, and standards-setting organizations in several other countries prescribe standards that govern the content and definition of items on a statement of financial performance (an income statement in business accounting) and financial status (a balance sheet). They publish rules for measuring each item in these reports as well as for how these items should be presented. For example, most monetary assets are reported at their fair value, but most nonmonetary assets are reported at their historical cost, adjusted in some cases for depreciation. Preparers must adhere to these rules in the published financial statements.

Banks, insurance companies, and other regulated companies must prepare financial statements required by regulators; they do not necessarily have to conform to GAAP standards. Organizations in an industry may use accounting practices recommended by an industry association. Many accounting numbers are used for management purposes, and that management accounting information need not follow GAAP. For example, most companies keep a record of sales orders when they are received, but GAAP requires the recognition of sales revenue only when the goods are shipped or the services are rendered.

A state legislature may require financial reports for its local governments that are prepared according to its specifications, but those specifications are not necessarily aligned with GAAP.

Similarly, an agency that makes a grant to a municipality may require whatever information it wishes. If the municipality does not provide the information, it loses the grant. Organizations that receive grants from the federal government must conform to the requirements in the Single Audit Act. Compliance is assumed unless there is a report to the contrary.

Many users of business financial statements are investors. They decide whether to buy, sell, or hold securities partly on the basis of the audited financial statements. Taxpayers do not make a comparable decision; they must pay taxes, whatever they are. Both business and governments have bond issues, but the bonds of many local governments are issued through a state agency, and individuals do not need information about the municipality. In general, therefore, users of government general-purpose financial statements in the United States need much less detail than do users of business financial statements.

A government accounting standard should describe the format and content of general-purpose financial statements. Statement 34 describes a complete accounting system, including management accounting and bookkeeping procedure. This is too much. Paragraphs that are unrelated to general-purpose financial statements should be deleted.

Some people congratulate the GASB for making available more government financial information than ever before. They point out that organizations develop "data warehouses," and computers can locate quickly any item in these warehouses.[8] Individual organizations are indeed storing much more data than they did in previous years. However, the new systems take time and money to develop. Many data are unique to an organization. It is highly unlikely that the GASB or any other standards-setting organization will be able to develop a set of principles to cover this much detail. The GASB should not try.

Some may disagree with my conclusion that Statement 34 is too detailed. They may say that it is better to have too much information than not enough. My response is that the GASB is charged with the difficult job of issuing standards for general-purpose financial statements and should not try to tackle more than is necessary. Other standards setters have not done that. For example, "gross margin" is an important number in many businesses, but the FASB does not require that it be reported.

Unnecessary Detail

A stated purpose of fund accounting is "accountability"; that is, accounting should report whether resources were used legally for the stated purpose. As was pointed out above, the government-wide system does this on an exception basis. If an organization has not adhered to legal or grantor requirements, that fact is reported. Usually the accounts will not show such an error; management makes sure the accounts show adherence to the legal requirements. Auditors may report noncompliance in a certain fund if their examination reveals that the amounts were incorrect. Fund accounting reports the facts about every important fund even though in most cases all of them will be in compliance. In business organizations such information is collected when it is required. If accountability is taken literally, there is no need to report funds that are in compliance.

States, the federal government, and other entities that provide resources with legal limitations on how those funds are to be spent may require reports on the details of spending. These are special-purpose reports, not parts of the general-purpose financial statements.

Conclusion

The system described in Statement 34 and its subsequent modifications are intolerable. There will be two sets of financial statements with different numbers for the bottom line of the income statement (labeled "Changes in Net Assets") and for individual items. An accounting standards board should prescribe the best financial statement. It should not describe two quite different sets of statements and require organizations to publish both.

The usually neutral American Institute of Certified Public Accountants has summed up the general public opinion in the title of its booklet on the subject, *How in the GASB Are We Going to Do This?*

The government system should be similar in most respects to the business accounting system. The "fund accounting" alternative is archaic. The information needed about separate funds can be obtained easily from a business-type system;

business have funds (e.g., advance payments, employee with-holdings) whose use is restricted to a specified purpose.

Compared with a business of similar size, preparing a report on the financial performance and status of a municipality should be relatively simple, and understanding such a report should be relatively easy. A municipality is located in one well-defined geographic place, and the accountant usually does not deal with income taxes, foreign exchange, tariffs, or national customs. Municipal managers try to attract new tax-payers, but those marketing efforts are trivial compared with those of a company that sells branded products. The cost of a municipality's services, the size of its workforce, and its physical resources are similar from one year to the next. Management may deal with storms, floods, crime waves, fires, and other unanticipated needs, but these events occur relatively infrequently. The amount of resources needed next year can be estimated fairly accurately this year. A municipality obtains most of those resources from taxpayers; collecting taxes is easier than generating and collecting receivables in most businesses. Municipalities have adopted new management accounting tools, but those tools are not included in general-purpose financial statements.

Notes

[1] Gains are included in revenues because for the purpose of this analysis there is no reason to discuss them separately. Gains have the same effect as other revenues on interperiod equity. Similarly, losses are included in expenses.

[2] Revenues are described in paragraphs 47 through 55 of Statement 34 and are the subject of Statement 33. This list is not the same as the list in those paragraphs because I believe nonoperating resource inflows are not consistent with the concept of revenue that is implicit in the interperiod equity concept. The reasons for this distinction are given in a later section. Paragraph 16 of Statement 34 requires that revenue be recognized "in accordance with the requirement of Statement No. 33." Paragraph 29 of Statement 33 requires that property taxes be recognized when they "become available and measurable," and paragraph 30(b) repeats this. This principle seems to be inconsistent with the revenue principles inherent in interperiod equity. Property taxes, like other receivables, are revenue in the period to which they apply, less an allowance for bad debts.

[3] Expenses are described in paragraphs 41 through 46 of Statement 34. This list is not exactly the same as the list in those paragraphs because I believe that depreciation on contributed capital assets is not an expense. The reasons for this are given in a later section.

[4] "Efficiency" is the ratio of effort to outputs. Effort is often synonymous with expenses, but accounting does not provide information about the outputs of specific activities. An acceptable measure of the output of the whole organization is revenue, but many individual activities have no revenue. "Effectiveness" is a measure of output, which cannot be measured for the organization as a whole.

[5] If the rule for debits to the capital project funds differs from the rule for debits to construction in progress in the government-wide system, the government-wide treatment should govern. Its rules are used widely for this purpose.

[6] See, for example, Marc Robinson, "Measuring Compliance with the Golden Rule," *Fiscal Studies*, November 1998.

[7] In a 1997 article a former chairman of the FASB gave reasons against creating a separate governmental board. See Douglas J. Kirk, "Commentary on Jurisdictional Conflict and Conceptual Differences in Standards Setting: FASB and GASB," *Accounting Horizons*, December 1997, pp. 107–113.

[8] Michael H. Granof commends the GASB for requiring what he calls a "data warehouse." I believe governments should indeed add to the data they maintain, but the bulk of those data are for management accounting and other uses that are not related to general-purpose financial statements. "Governmental Accounting and Reporting: A Data Warehousing Approach," *Government Accountants Journal*, Summer 1999, pp. 30–38.

9

IMPLEMENTATION

This chapter has two main sections. The first section describes the efforts required to implement the suggestions made in previous chapters. The second section recommends an organizational arrangement for carrying out that work.

Suggested Changes

This section describes (1) the major changes from current practice, (2) changes that are described earlier in this text, (3) current projects of the Financial Accounting Standards Board (FASB), and (4) other changes.

Substantive Changes

I propose only three substantive suggestions that have not been incorporated already in FASB texts: (1) the solvency statement described in Chapter 3, (2) recognition of the cost of using equity capital, and (3) a clearer definition of net income.

Solvency Statement. Because individual balance sheet items no longer are reported according to the same measurement rules, I recommend replacing the balance sheet with a solvency statement. Like the balance sheet, this statement includes all current assets, other financial assets, current liabilities, other liabilities, and sources of equity capital. The solvency statement eliminates fixed assets. Solvency statements already are used in the law.

Cost of Using Equity Capital. The principal difference between financial accounting and economics accounting is that financial accounting does not report the cost of using equity capital. There are some problems determining how this cost should be measured, but the same principles already are used in economics.

Definition of Net Income. The Enron debacle and other financial fiascoes have demonstrated the need to clarify the definition of net income. Financial Accounting Standard (FAS) 2 dealt with this problem in 1975 for research and development organizations and many standards since that time have added details to this rule; however, there has been no attempt to redefine the generalization that takes these details into account.

Much of the current controversy involves this concept. Refining the definition of net income may solve most of the apparent problems.

I recommend limiting the definition of net income to financial accounting matters. Management accounting topics should not be dealt with.

The papers about accounting standards that were referred to in Chapter 1 can be disregarded. They are so general that they have no bearing on the standards themselves. Testimony in the hearings on the recent fiascoes contains very little information about practical steps that can be taken to correct the deficiencies.

Editorial Changes

Other than the specific suggestions in Chapters 3 through 8, the changes I suggest can be implemented easily. They are in effect editorial; that is, they can be implemented without debate over accounting principles. The accounting rules are now described in more than 2,000 pages. The following suggestions will reduce the bulk of these rules greatly. State and local governments may be required to use different rules by the legislature; if that is the case, those differences must be accepted. However, they are legislative, not financial accounting, requirements.

Taxonomy

Editing the existing rules is a huge, time-consuming task, but there is relatively little disagreement about what should be done.

The existing structure of financial accounting provides an overall method for arriving at a satisfactory structure. The categories are asset, liability, equity, revenue, and expense. All accounting numbers fit within one of those categories. The effort should lead to a set of accounting rules that fit within a hierarchy with one of those names at the top.

The format already published by the XBRL Project committee is an excellent beginning. Although the committee has no authority, the team's hope is that companies will adopt its taxonomy voluntarily. As of April 2003 there are about 200 current XBRL members including software firms, individual companies, governments, banks, and accounting firms. Many foreign governments are considering adoption of the XBRL taxonomy. It is being encouraged by the SEC in its EDGAR Online, Inc. (Source: XBRL Progress Report, April 2003). Since many accounting systems are devised by a few major consulting firms, it is likely that consultants for those firms will recommend the taxonomy be adopted.

Details of the Effort.   The development of a taxonomy is a complicated task, as is explained below.

- It involves arriving at definitions for each of the items listed.
- The number of items should be limited to the number that will

fit on one page of a Statement of Financial Status, an Income Statement, and a Statement of Changes in Equity.

- The standards should be limited to the elements listed in those statements. It should not include any explanation, management discussion of those elements, historical background, basis for conclusions, benefits and costs, or arguments for and against any standard. These topics may be described in a separate document. This should reduce the current standards by approximately two-thirds.

- There should be a definition of each item in sufficient detail to account for all the details that currently are reported.

- Poets love synonyms; standards setters should avoid them. An individual who reads about net income in one sentence and profit in the next sentence has a right to assume that there is something different in the messages of those two sentences. Synonyms exist in standards because the people who developed the standards had different personal tastes. Such standards are sloppy and confusing; indeed, one definition of a synonym is "almost the same as another word in the same language."

- The standards should describe the content of each item.

- No auditing standards should be included. That is a separate topic with a separate approach to the development of standards.

- Approximately 10 standards relate to specific industries rather than to the economy as a whole. The taxonomy should determine whether these items require a special section in the standards or can be melded into existing standards. It may not be possible to fit into a single hierarchy all the industries, including oil and gas-producing companies, real estate, timber, insurance, news, and entertainment. The editor will have to work out a solution to this problem.

- All aspects of a topic should be discussed together. Rules relating to leasing illustrate the inadequacy of the FASB's structure. These rules are found in eight standards, ten technical bulletins, six interpretations, and 20 rulings of the Emerging Issues Task Force. Such a hodgepodge often is found in a topic whose rules have existed for a long time and constitutes an obvious reason to examine them.

- The terms should fit into this hierarchy. Because the term for the bottom line is "net income," an intermediate measure should qualify the term in a label that contains the word "income." The term for the difference between operating revenues and operating expenses should be "operating income." The item labeled "income," for instance, should always reflect the sum or difference of at least two components. "Interest income" is not a proper term even though it is used in income tax regulations; it is not a total. The term should be "interest revenue."

Taxonomy is similar to a typical chart of accounts, which most companies have. Each company's chart of accounts should include the items listed in the taxonomy. It also would contain details for each item that is useful for management purposes.

In the chart of accounts individual items are listed in the order in which they appear on the financial statements. Each reported line on a financial statement is a summary of many numbers that relate to it. For example, a large company may have thousands of customers, each of which has an amount of accounts receivable as of the end of the accounting period. The balance sheet reports this total, often with an offsetting allowance for bad debts.

The XBRL labels provide only the first few fields of the accounts.

The account number for a transaction that increases accounts receivable would reflect a hierarchy of items. Consider the number of the following:

Field   1 2 3
Account number   1 2 3 5, etc.

This number means the following:

- It is an asset.
- It is a current asset.
- It is an accounts receivable.

"Etc." may specify the customer account number, the date of the transaction, and perhaps other information.

The resulting account number may have 20 digits or more, but much of it can be entered automatically. The first three fields of a number for the sale of an item in a store may be contained in a register, and the customer's credit card is inserted to obtain the customer number.

An account number like this applies to every transaction incurred in a company. These transactions automatically become part of the items in the fields described above.

A small problem: The U.S. XBRL is 12 digits long, and in other countries it is 13 digits. There should be a single code worldwide.

The complexities of these accounts may not be fully appreciated. Dennis Beresford, former chairman of the FASB, has stated that "the FASB Emerging Issues Task Force has been wrestling for some time with the topic of 'Revenue Arrangements with Multiple Deliverables.'"

The XBRL rules will supersede the taxonomy of Lexis, Standard & Poor's, EDGAR, Bloomberg, and all other existing databases. However, those sources will continue to publish summaries.

An important advantage of this approach is that higher definitions in the hierarchy usually govern the items listed below them. This avoids the problem of defining a term, such as "asset," in several accounting standards. Additionally, it provides a numbering system that must be used by all organizations. Companies then expand their account numbers to provide the details they wish to report. The FASB chart of accounts need list only the numbers in the balance sheet (or solvency statement) and the income statement. The amounts appearing in the other two required statements—the Statement of Changes in Equity and the Cash Flow Statement—are simply rearrangements of those numbers. Ideally, the FASB should require the use of this taxonomy, but this would involve so many detailed problems that early recognition is unlikely.

Because only the current rules will be listed, finding what

certain rules were on an earlier date may pose a problem. The solution may be to publish a set of standards each year.

The text for a rule should describe the rule and in some cases give examples of how it should be implemented, but that is all it should do. These explanations are appropriately published separately, as is the case with explanations accompanying laws; they do not help in understanding the rules.

There should be no reference to "pro forma financial statements," as is recommended in the document "Impact of the Current Economic and Business Environment on Financial Reporting" prepared by the large accounting firms. These statements are not generally accepted accounting principles (GAAP) and never will be.

With XBRL the data are entered once and thereafter are automatically a part of financial statements, EDGAR filings, the IRS tax filing, and other special reports such as a loan document. Some people recommend that financial statements be made available more rapidly than they are at present—even at the same time as the events being reported. Organizations spend much time deciding on amounts to be reported, especially those which involve estimates. The idea of "real-time" reports is unrealistic.

The sciences are in the process of developing a system called Internet 2 which can provide a way to store vast amounts of information within a single system. The financial accounting system is one of the most widely used measurement systems in the world. It might benefit by setting up its own Internet 3 system, although this probably is for some time in the future.

Organizing the Review

Nature of the Changes

Some of the changes suggested here are substantive, and others are editorial. The two types require different skills for implementation. The tasks involved in making the two types of changes are quite different. A committee must be created to supervise these changes.

If there is disagreement about the meaning of a standard, the matter should be referred to the overall committee. Publishers of encyclopedias and reference texts face this problem and solve it effectively. They select an editor who assembles a staff to produce the finished product.

The review covers topics under the jurisdiction of the FASB and the Governmental Accounting Standards Board (GASB). Therefore, it should cover both boards.

Some rule-making organizations identify and implement major improvements in their rules in a special study that is undertaken once in a generation. Such studies are difficult and complicated and require skills different from those needed to develop standards. The FASB's concepts and standards have been developed over a period of 25 years, a longer interval than reviews of earlier standards. Pronouncements by the board's predecessor, the Accounting Principles Board (APB), were examined by the Wheat Committee 15 years after the APB began to function. Standards developed by the International Accounting Standards Board (IASB) were revised in 1997, 20 years after the IASB began to function. These intervals suggest that a revision of the FASB and GASB rules is now appropriate.

As was pointed out in Chapter 1, criticism of FASB pronouncements is increasing.

Editing

The earlier chapters in this book listed dozens, perhaps hundreds, of items that would be revised if these suggestions were adapted. The resulting changes would include the use of a single taxonomy to replace the synonyms found in the current concepts and standards, the deletion of unnecessary information, the rearrangement of the material into a logical order in accordance with the taxonomy, and the deletion of the separate standards on nonprofits and state and local government organizations and incorporation of their substance into the general standard.

Most of the hundreds of pages of appendixes to the existing standards can be disregarded; they are a history of the activities leading to the standards and an explanation of why certain standards were adopted. In a few cases those materials can be included. They help clarify what a standard means and may be included for that purpose, as is the case with many federal statues.

The result will be one set of standards for business organizations, nonprofit organizations, and state and local governments. There is no need to separate these three types of activities, as is now done.

This project would not deal with standards that are unique to certain industries, such as the industries described below. After the overall set of standards is complete, particular industry standards can be changed by means of a separate effort to simplify them while relying on the new rules for financial accounting in general. Including industry standards in the taxonomy may require a special arrangement.

The XBRL Project has made an excellent beginning in this direction, but the XBRL committee has no power of enforcement. Its efforts so far represent only a first step.

Resurrecting Previous Standards

Cash Flow Statement.   FAS95, the FASB's rules for cash flow statements, superseded earlier rules for those statements that had been used for many years. It recommends the "direct" method rather than the "indirect" method used in Accounting Principles Board (APB) Opinion 19. The word "direct" sounds more credible, but a large majority of the individuals who use the statement continue to employ the indirect method. There are sound reasons for this preference. The new cash flow statement is confusing and is less informative than its predecessor. Therefore, the predecessor should be resurrected.

Comprehensive Income. FAS130 requires a statement of comprehensive income that includes some items excluded from the current income statement. I see no need for a statement with this additional information. It is already reported in the statement of changes in equity and does not emphasize the important distinction between net income and other changes in equity. This topic was discussed in Chapter 5.

Nonprofit Accounting. The only difference between standards for nonprofit organizations and standards for businesses is that nonprofit organizations have rules for reporting the cost of equity capital and businesses do not. These rules were used by nonprofit organizations before the acceptance of FAS116 and 117. FASB pronouncements on nonprofit organizations should be deleted, and the method previously used for contributed capital should be resurrected.

Revenues, expenses, and the resulting net income should have the same definitions in nonprofit organizations that they have in businesses. The differences arise because nonprofit numbers are used differently, not because they are derived differently. In business, the higher the net income, the better the entity's financial performance. In nonprofit organizations, the ideal net income number is slightly higher than zero on average. A lower number signals that the entity has not broken even financially, the same meaning that it has in business. A higher number indicates that the entity has not provided services to students, patients, and others it seeks to serve. But this does not affect the way the numbers are calculated.

Concepts Statement (CON) 6, "Elements of Financial Statements," classifies transactions for nonprofit organizations into three categories: unrestricted, temporarily restricted, and permanently restricted. As was explained in Chapter 7, this classification is not useful. Transactions in nonbusiness organizations should be classified as either operating or contributed capital. This was the practice before CON 6 was issued. The FASB maintains that its nonprofit standards must be consistent with CON 6.

Nonprofit organizations constitute an "industry," just as public utilities, insurance agencies, and financial institutions are industries. As is the case with these other industries, separate standards are necessary only for transactions that differ from those of general business.

These valid differences relate to differences in the source of additions to equity. Business organizations receive additions to equity from their owners, whereas nonprofit organizations receive additions to equity from contributors.[1] (Both types of organizations receive capital in the form of retained earnings.) Special standards for nonprofit organizations are needed only for contributed capital transactions.

The standards for nonprofit organizations are given in FAS116 and 117. Unfortunately, they are defective. The rules used by nonprofit organizations before the publication of CON 6 are much better. There were minor differences in the rules for individual industries—colleges and universities, hospitals, and other nonprofit organizations—but those rules made the basic distinction between operating activities and contributed capital. The inconsistencies among the earlier rules are minor and easy to correct.

State and Local Government.   When the Financial Accounting Foundation (FAF) accepted jurisdiction for developing non-business standards, there was an implicit assumption that those standards would be developed by the FASB. This is what happened for nonprofit organizations. For state and local government organizations, however, a new organization was created: the Governmental Accounting Standards Board. It was created only because some government people threatened to continue using the existing National Council on Governmental Accounting Standards if the FASB was made responsible for developing government standards.

I doubt that this threat was serious. If it had been carried out, it could have been countered by a statement by the American Institute of Certified Public Accountants designating the FASB as the only authoritative body. Users of government accounting information, especially those who invest in government bonds, would use FASB standards; so would certified public accountants. However, the FAF decided to avoid this threat by creating the GASB. The GASB took almost 15 years to develop an overall framework for governmental accounting. The resulting Statement No. 34 describes an excellent set of standards for state and local governments that is based on business concepts. Unfortunately, it also requires government organizations to publish two sets of financial statements: one for accrual accounting, called the government-wide system, and one for the existing fund accounting. The amounts reported for the same transactions in these statements differ, and that makes no sense.

The 50 paragraphs on fund accounting should be deleted. Standards for the treatment of contributed capital assets are needed, but they are essentially the same as those used for nonprofit organizations.

Eliminating fund accounting will be easy, although probably painful. The tremendous detail specified in Statement 34 can be condensed easily; the editing procedure involves primarily deletion, not rewriting. The corrections will not be made, however, unless the GASB is persuaded to make them, and this will require strong requests from interested parties.

As for the GASB, there is little reason now to continue it. A compromise solution is to keep the GASB but limit its work to performance measurement and other topics that do not affect financial accounting standards. Additionally, it could be responsible for the important task of teaching government accountants how to understand and use the FASB standards.

Current FASB Studies

Current FASB studies include complicated securities, business combinations, nonprofit combinations, special purpose entities (SPEs), disclosure of intangible assets, fair value, net income, guarantees, liabilities and equity, acquisitions of certain financial institutions, and revenue recognition.

I do not deal with transactions now discussed by the FASB because I do not know the outcome of these studies. I also do not discuss FASB standards beginning with FAS136. Some transactions do not report "arm's-length" amounts. For other transactions there is no true marketplace. In one type, for example, the buyer implicitly agrees to give back the goods in the next accounting period, so there should be no real revenue recognizing a sale. Such a practice inflates the seller's revenue in the current period.

In stock option transactions there is no "buyer"; the value of the option is whatever the "seller" chooses to select. In other transactions the buyer and the seller are the same individual acting in two different capacities. In ordinary sales transactions, the seller decides that the price is a fair use of resources and the buyer agrees that the amount is a fair use of his or her outflows. Otherwise there would not be a transaction. Many transactions involving financial instruments have these characteristics.

The FASB has initiated a project as described below:

> "The FASB agreed to launch a series of administrative projects aimed at codifying and simplifying the U.S. accounting literature. This overall project is being initiated in response to concerns raised by constituents about the quantity, complexity and lack of easy retrievability of the body of U.S. accounting literature, including guidance issued by the EITF, the American Institute of Certified Public Accountants (AICPA) and the SEC. A key objective of this project is to improve the usability and effectiveness of that literature.
>
> "[T]he FASB hopes to partner with others in developing an online database that will include all of the U.S. accounting literature."[2]

The FASB seems to accept much of the existing wording rather than the major rearrangement that I suggest.

Other Recent Proposals

Financial Executives International, the leading association of finance officers, recently offered a set of accounting proposals. This group proposes that financial executives should have a code of ethical conduct, companies should promote ethical behavior, and financial officers should have knowledge of finance. It also recommends creating a new oversight body for the accounting industry, restricting the nonaudit services performed by independent auditors, restricting the hiring of personnel from the external auditor, creating a committee to reform the FASB, improving financial statements by means of better management discussion and analysis, ensuring that all audit committees have accounting knowledge, continuing professional education for audit committee members, rotating audit committee chairs about every five years, and disclosing governance report practices. These recommendations are broad generalizations. None refer to reforming financial accounting rules.[3]

The chairman of the board of the American Institute of Certified Public Accountants (AICPA) had a list of recommendations, but they were much broader than improving financial accounting rules.[4]

Other organizations had similar views. A recent survey conducted by Financial Executives International had 216 responses to its survey on the complexity of accounting rules. There was general agreement that the rules were complex. However, there was disagreement about whether they were complex because business financial instruments had become complex or because they were unnecessarily complicated.[5]

There is no doubt that business instruments have become increasingly complex, and the rules must deal with those complications.

Financial Accounting Foundation

Every year the FAF conducts a review of accounting standards. However, its analyses have been superficial. The FAF has not recommended any substantial changes in the existing standards.

The FAF, through the FASB, is responsible for establishing financial accounting standards. Although the Securities and Exchange Commission (SEC) is also responsible, it has relied on the FASB for all its decisions. The SEC participates actively in all proposed changes in financial accounting standards.

A new FAF committee should be organized for the major analysis proposed here. The committee members should not serve full-time because the leaders in the field cannot be expected to give up their current positions. The committee should have a staff, but it should not come from the FASB since it would be scrutinizing the work of the FASB. Several federal organizations, such as the National Science Foundation and the National Institutes of Health, have such committees.

As the previous analysis indicates, the new FAF committee would have two quite different tasks. One would be to change accounting standards to a hierarchy similar to that made by the XBRL. The task of developing a new hierarchy is huge. It should be contracted to a firm skilled in similar work. This could be the management side of an accounting firm or one of the organizations that now do similar work, such as Standard and Poor's, Bloomberg, and Lexis-Nexus. The other task would be to develop new basic standards. The AICPA has created committees to do this work, and those committees should become subcommittees of the new FAF committee. Two possible alternatives to a new FAF committee have been suggested: the Public Company Accounting Oversight Board and the International Accounting Standards Board.

The Public Company Accounting Oversight Board

The Public Company Accounting Oversight Board has five full-time members appointed by the SEC, as established by the Sarbanes-Oxley Act of 2002.

The board is responsible for "auditing, quality control,

ethics, independence, and other standards related to the preparation of audit reports for issuers." This group has the authority to amend, modify, repeal, and reject any new standards. Many functions of this board are already functions of the SEC.

International Accounting Standards Board

The International Accounting Standards Board (IASB) is another possibility. It develops worldwide standards. However, I doubt that there would be support in the United States for acceptance of those standards as such.

Notes

[1] A nonprofit organization does have an owner, usually its governing board.

[2] FASB Financial Accounting Series, Codification and Simplication Projects, February 2002.

[3] Financial Executives International, "FEI Observations and Recommendations, Improving Financial Management, Financial Reporting and Corporate Governance," March 2002.

[4] The AICPA's recommendations are as follows: improve the financial reporting model; revise rules for SPEs; require additional disclosures, especially with the management discussion and analysis section; require reporting on an internal control system; require additional effort by auditors; require additional information on future developments; reporting frequency and penalize corporate officials for withholding material information. James G. Castellano, Chairman of AICPA Board, "Restoring Public Confidence," *Journal of Accountancy*, April 2002.

[5] FEI Research Foundation, *Financial Reporting Complexity, Survey Looks for Solutions*, January 2002.

10

FEDERAL ACCOUNTING STANDARDS

Currently, financial accounting standards for the federal government are established by the Federal Accounting Standards Advisory Board (FASAB). In 1990 the FASAB issued rules for a modern accounting system for the federal government. The system was to be implemented in 1997. It has not been implemented. In my opinion, it never will be implemented as presently constituted.

In this chapter I describe the evidence that the FASAB standards won't work, the reasons for that failure, and what needs to be done to have a successful system.

The FASAB accounting rules should be analyzed at two levels. At the level of the government as a whole, the purpose of those rules is the same as the purpose of the Financial Accounting Standards Board (FASB) rules for businesses and nonprofit organizations. The accounting systems prescribed by the board are intended to provide comparable information about the financial status and performance of the organizations within its jurisdiction. However, there is only one federal government, and so there is no possible comparability except with prior years. I believe that information reported on the FASAB balance sheet is not worth the cost of its collection. The Treasury Department has excellent data about the financial status of the government as a whole, and Congress has data about appropriations.

At the second level the FASAB rules govern the accounting information used by individual agencies. In businesses and nonbusiness organizations such rules are called management accounting rules. They differ from the financial accounting rules, that is, the rules for financial reports to outside parties. The FASAB rules for agencies in the federal government should be judged on the criterion of how well they meet management and congressional needs.

Background

The history of federal government accounting is a story of attempts by several commissions and similar organizations to shift accounting for operating activities from an obligation (i.e., appropriation) basis to an expense basis, but the House Appropriations Committees have always succeeded in killing those attempts. I start this section with a description of those bases.

Obligation Accounting and Expense Accounting

Throughout the twentieth century and into the twenty-first the House Appropriations Committee has been responsible for legislation that appropriates funds for the operating costs of government agencies. (Because the rules for reporting and controlling capital expenditures are different from the rules for operating costs, I do not discuss them here.) This legislation is expressed as obligation authority. An "obligation" is the amount stated in a contract between the government and a vendor or an employee to provide goods or services. "Obligation authority" is the dollar limit of the amounts that are authorized for the budget year. With the obligation system, the contracts or employment authorizations state the specific amount authorized. The task of keeping spending within the authorized limit is easy; a contracting officer who signs a contract that exceeds the authorized amount is by law required to repay the excess personally. This penalty is spelled out in the Anti-Deficiency Act (R.S. 3679). Consequently, the authorization rarely is exceeded. Most violations are the result of a clerical error and are forgiven.[1]

Expense accounting focuses on resources (labor, materials, purchase services) consumed by responsibility centers within an agency. This is the focus that businesses use in reporting and controlling resources consumed. Expenses for employees consist of the compensation (salaries, pensions, and other benefits). Expenses for supplies are the cost of the supplies used during the year. Expenses for purchased services (utilities, maintenance, travel, and outside experts) are the costs of the services received by the responsibility center during the year.

The following examples illustrate the difference between expense accounting and obligation accounting:

- A contract made in 2001 by an officer at the Naval Supply Depot in Mechanicsburg, Pennsylvania, to buy widgets for use at the Charlestown Navy Yard in 2002 is a Mechanicsburg obligation in 2001; it is a Charlestown expense in 2002.[2]
- A contract signed in 2001 to paint a building is an obligation in 2001. If the building is painted in 2002, it is a 2002 expense. A contract signed in 2001 for travel costs is an obligation for 2001. If the trip is made in 2002, it is a 2002 expense.
- In the obligation focus, the cost of a "borrowed" employee (an employee who temporarily works for an agency other than his or her home agency) is reported by the agency to which the employee is permanently assigned. In expense accounting, the agency that uses the services of the employee is charged for his or her compensation cost.

Expense accounting reports the costs of resources used and matches those costs with the results obtained. The responsibility center manager who authorizes the use of those resources is accountable for their cost and for the work accomplished. Comparing expenses with the results obtained is a useful measure of efficiency in many responsibility centers. Even if there is no valid, quantitative measure of results, the comparison of actual expenses with budgeted amounts is an important measure of performance. An expense system is much more useful than an obligation system to managers who plan, budget, and then make decisions and evaluate their own performance. It is also very useful to those who supervise the responsibility center managers.

Expense accounting also provides a better basis for preparing budgets. The cost of the amount of work planned for the year can be obtained by multiplying the planned number of units of work to be accomplished by the estimated cost per unit.

An obligation system can easily result in inefficiencies. If the obligation authority exists, the amount specified in a contract can be charged to it even if all the contractual goods or services are not actually needed. In an expense system, unnecessary expenses are less likely to be incurred. The amount of actual expense (that is, the resources used or consumed) can be compared with the budgeted expense, which is the units of work accomplished multiplied by the expense per unit.

A "Beetle Bailey" comic strip is my favorite example of the basic defect in an obligation system. Lieutenant Fuzz is in a staff meeting called by General Halftrack. In the first panel Fuzz reports with obvious pleasure, "Sir, the battalion will have $281 left over for the remainder of the fiscal year." General Halftrack responds, "So?" Fuzz says, "I thought you'd like to send it back to Washington so they can give it back to the people." The final panel shows Lieutenant Fuzz sitting in the corner, bound and gagged, as General Halftrack asks, "Any more reports?".

Most business and nonprofit organizations use expense-based systems. The government systems of many other countries, including Canada, the United Kingdom, Australia, and

New Zealand, have expense-based systems. Municipal and state governments do not now use expense-based systems, but Statement 34 of the Governmental Accounting Standards Board requires that they do so beginning in 2003.[3]

In recent years the obligation system has been broadened somewhat. Some agencies now include employee fringe benefits as part of authorized employee costs. Some agencies charge the cost of borrowed employees to the office that uses them. Also, as will be described below, some costs are held initially in working capital funds and later are charged to the responsibility center that used the resources. However, these are exceptions to the general rule.

Working Capital Funds

A working capital fund is a device for holding costs in suspense in the interval between the time and place in which they are obligated and the time and place in which they are expensed. It therefore permits some expense items to be reported within an obligation system. The costs of some services initially are recorded as an addition to a working capital fund by the responsibility center that provides the services and become an expense to the center that uses the services. The motor pool is an example. In the 1960s, under my direction, the Department of Defense created working capital funds. In the first year they totaled $5 billion.

The applicability of working capital funds is limited, however. The Department of Defense's effort to develop a Defense Business Operations Fund (DBOF) represented an attempt to use working capital funds more broadly than is practicable. Established in October 1991, the DBOF accounted for annual operating costs of support and overhead activities of $77 billion. The fund was supposed to charge the cost of those activities to the responsibility centers that used the services.

In August 1995 the DBOF fund manager admitted that costs of $16 *billion* could not be traced to the agencies that received the services. The system never produced reliable reports for the managers of support and overhead activities and the managers of the responsibility centers that received the services. On December 11, 1996, the DBOF was discontinued. The lesson learned from this experience is that the working capital fund devices will work only for inventories of consumable items, such as supplies and clothing, and for services such as commissary and motor pools.

History

Shortly after the U.S. republic was founded, the Treasury Department began keeping records of cash receipts and disbursements, the resulting assets and liabilities, and the status of appropriated funds. Agencies had their own management accounting systems, but the Treasury records were the only government-wide financial records until the General Accounting Office (GAO) was created in 1921.

The GAO is responsible for auditing all government accounts. Until World War II it required agencies to send their records to Washington for auditing. That practice became unworkable in the 1940s because of the tremendous volume created by World War II; the documents awaiting audit filled a huge warehouse. Consequently, the GAO transferred audit responsibility to the agencies. Each agency now has its own internal audit organization, which audits the agency records from field offices; this is the same practice businesses use.

In 1947 the GAO established an Accounting Systems Division.

First Hoover Commission. The report of the first Hoover Commission (1949) recommended that the federal system be changed to expense accounting. Many of its recommendations were controversial, however, and a law mandating expense accounting was not enacted.

At that time I was working in the Department of Defense. The assistant secretaries of the army, navy, and air force asked the Assistant Secretary of Defense (Comptroller) what they should do to implement the Hoover Commission's recommendations. The oral answer was "Nothing."

In 1950 the Budget and Accounting Procedures Act made the GAO responsible for developing accounting principles. One of the requirements of the act was that agency systems be placed on an expense basis. The GAO Accounting Systems Division helped several agencies—on a voluntary basis—develop expense accounting systems, but agencies were not required to do so. There was no government-wide expense system.

Second Hoover Commission.   The second Hoover Commission (1955) also recommended expense accounting. That led to Public Law 84-863 in 1956, requiring agencies to install expense systems "as soon as practicable." That legislation was sponsored by the House Government Operations Committee. Two federal agencies then submitted budgets on an expense basis. The House Appropriations Committee rejected both budgets without comment. That was the end of expense accounting. Public Law 84-863 is still on the books.

The GAO's responsibility was reinforced by the Federal Managers' Financial Integrity Act of 1982 (U.S.C. 3512). In 1984 the GAO published a policy and procedures manual, Title 2, which contained a chart of accounts that was several hundred pages long.

Other Developments.   Although there was no legislation for many years, several actions relating to expense accounting were taken:

- In the Department of Defense (DoD) each of the three services developed accounting systems that reported expenses.
- In the 1960s the DoD developed a defensewide system that reported both obligations and expenses. I received a citation for this work from the Federal Government Accountants Association. Two days before the banquet at which the citation was to be presented the House Appropriations Committee issued a

letter stating that no additional funds would be authorized to test the system. That was its demise.

- When the Bureau of the Budget became the Office of Management and Budget, its new management division was made responsible for developing management accounting systems. That division had some success in persuading agencies to adopt expense accounting systems for internal purposes even though it had no authority to require this.
- The Joint Financial Management Improvement Program is a small organization that was formed in 1948. It exchanges ideas among the agencies and works with some agencies in developing expense accounting systems.
- Beginning in the 1980s, the Comptroller General issued a set of financial statements for the federal government. Those statements were derived from adjustments made to available information from various sources, not from actual journal entries. (Comptroller General Charles Bowsher was responsible for introducing those statements, and his influence was important in the FASB's decision to require financial statements for the government as a whole.)
- In 1993 the Vice President's *Report of the National Performance Review* recommended that an expense accounting system be developed (Gore, 1993).
- FASAB standards were accepted as authoritative by the American Institute of Certified Public Accountants in October 1999.

Federal Accounting Standards Advisory Board

The Federal Accounting Standards Advisory Board was created in 1990 by the heads of the three agencies responsible for developing accounting systems: the General Accounting Office, the Treasury Department, and the Office of Management and Budget.

The Government Management Reform Act of 1994 required the FASAB to develop a system that would produce government-wide financial statements. The first such statements were to be those for fiscal year (FY) 1997.[4] This act was sponsored by the Senate Governmental Affairs Committee. The Federal Financial Management Improvement Act of 1996 strengthened the requirements.

The FASAB developed a system that reported *both* expenses and obligations; this is the current system. Congress authorizes money through the obligation system, and agencies obviously pay more attention to this "power of the purse" than to expense accounting, which has no corresponding support. Consequently, one wonders why the FASAB perpetuated the obligation system, which overshadows the expense system it was trying to promote. My guess is that Elmer Staats, the first chairman of the FASAB and one of the most astute individuals in Washington, decided that if obligation information was excluded, the House Appropriations Committee would oppose the FASAB legislation.

Failure of the FASAB System

In 1998 the Treasury Department issued the first set of government-wide financial statements derived from the FASAB system, that is, the fiscal 1997 statements. In its "opinion" letter on those statements, the Comptroller General stated,

> Because we were unable to determine the reliability of significant portions of the accompanying U.S. government's consolidated financial statements, we are unable to, and we do not, express an opinion on such consolidated financial statements. . . .
>
> As a result of material deficiencies in the government's systems, recordkeeping, documentation, and financial reporting, readers are cautioned that amounts reported in the consolidated financial statements and related notes may not be a reliable source of information. These material deficiencies also affect the reliability of certain information contained in the accompanying Management's Discussion and Analysis and any other financial management infor-

mation—including information used to manage the government day to day and budget information reported by agencies—which is taken from the same data sources as the consolidated financial statements.

The Comptroller General expanded on those weaknesses and problems in seven pages. Accountants call such a letter a "disclaimer." It is similar to a failing grade in school. If a listed business corporation received such a letter from its auditors (which happens extremely rarely), trading in its securities would be suspended immediately.

Financial statements are supposed to report an entity's financial status as of the end of a fiscal year and its financial performance during that year. The Comptroller General's letter said that these statements did not report either status or performance information. In other words, the statements are worthless.

The FY 1997 financial statements generated a few newspaper stories, journal mentions, and congressional testimony. As far as I know, not a single management or congressional office used those statements.

Similar financial statements were reported each year thereafter. Donald V. Hammond, Assistant Secretary of the Treasury, testified about the FY 1998 statements before a subcommittee of the House Government Reform Committee on March 31, 1999. Although it was expected that he would report progress in developing useful information, he did not describe a single item of information in the financial statements. Instead, his testimony mostly described implementation problems and promises to solve them (Hammond, 1999).

The Comptroller General's reports on each of the subsequent statements were also "disclaimer" letters, and there was even less interest than there had been earlier on the part of the media. The most favorable comment the Comptroller General could make was that more agencies were complying with the FASAB standards each year. However, he acknowledged that the numbers were far short of those needed to remove the disclaimer. A student who receives failing grades in all subjects in one semester and passes one of five subjects in the next semester has improved but is still a poor student.

The federal financial reports are not limited to the conventional items that usually are included in financial statements. Among the 118 pages in the FY 2000 report, about half contained interesting but nonfinancial information, such as the acreage of most grazing and forestry land for valuable resources on the continental shelf and many other items; in total those items probably exceed the monetary amount of the items that are listed on the balance sheet.

The GAO publishes annually a separate list of "high-risk" items: items that need special attention. For the last three years financial reporting has been on that list. Although more agencies have received unqualified audit opinions each year, most do not describe real improvement in their expense-based systems. In its FY 2000 report (page 121), the GAO stated,

> Many agencies have been able to obtain unqualified audit opinions only through heroic efforts, which include using extensive ad hoc procedures and billions of dollars in adjustments to derive numbers as of a single point in time—the end of the fiscal year. These efforts are often completed months after the end of the fiscal year. The fundamental problem is that agency financial systems cannot routinely provide this information.

Because an important purpose of the accounting system is to furnish information to management when it is needed, this practice demonstrates that the system is a failure in those agencies.

Public Notice.   The FASAB system presumably is the culmination of a 50-year effort to improve federal management by introducing an expense accounting system. That effort happened in the largest organization in the world. One would expect that there would be an outpouring of articles in magazines, newspapers, and industry journals applauding this victory. Although I have not studied all the sources, I have looked diligently for some mention and have not found any. Even the FASAB has not published or referred to success stories. The FASAB has a single message: More agencies are adopting the new system each year. As was pointed out above, that message is exaggerated. Several agencies have found a way to use obligation accounting to prepare expense-based financial statements by adjusting the obligation numbers for rough estimates of the percentage differences between obligations and expenses. Because these data do not come directly from an expense system, the statement that an increasing number of agencies are shifting to an expense basis is incorrect.

Causes of the FASAB's Failure

There are two unrelated reasons why the FASAB system has been a failure: (1) the continuation of the obligation system and (2) the FASAB system is too complicated.

Continuation of the Obligation System

As was mentioned earlier, the House Appropriations Committee appropriates funds on an obligation basis. Most other committees tolerate the obligation format; their proposals are easily stated in obligation terms. The Senate Governmental Affairs Committee has advocated an expense-based system, but this would be in addition to, not instead of, the obligation basis. Duplicative accounting systems are costly and confusing.

The fact that information in the congressional operating budget system conflicts with that in the FASAB system is the greatest weakness in the FASAB system. The power of the purse is an important power, and little attention is paid to a system that does not have it. A reasonable question is, Why has the FASAB tolerated the continued existence of the obligation system?

Congressional Level.   There are several reasons why Congress has not shifted its budget to an expense basis.

First, at the level of aggregation at which Congress works there is only a slight difference between obligation amounts and expense amounts. The important differences occur in agency responsibility centers. Therefore, there is little evidence at the congressional level that the obligation system should be scrapped. Budget analysts at the Office of Management and Budget (OMB) have the same attitude. Successive OMB assistant directors for management have tried to interest the director of OMB and the President in expense-based budgeting, but their efforts have not been successful.

Second, budgeteers in Congress and in the OMB are accustomed to the obligation system. They are highly competent people, and they wrestle with complicated problems. They have developed procedures for evaluating the thousands of proposed obligation line items. They will not accept a change to the expense basis unless they are convinced that the benefits of changing will be worth the considerable effort involved in learning how to analyze expense information. They do not recognize the management uses of expense information—information that managers in business companies regard as being essential.

Third, agency officials are well aware of the proverb "Don't bite the hand that feeds you." They believe it is in their best interest to concentrate on obtaining funds, not on persuading the House Appropriations Committee to change.

An expense system is a better control device than an obligation system. Actually, an expense-based system can permit tighter control. Control can be exercised over *both* obligations and expenses. Congress could legislate both a ceiling on an agency's total obligation authority and line items on an expense basis. The system can account for the movement of funds from obligations to expenses by using accounts for un-delivered orders and for inventories.[5]

Finally, I do not know of any accounting lobbyists. Not many people understand or care about the difference between expenses and obligations. Consequently, the advantages of an expense system do not interest many representatives, sena-tors, or their staffs.

Congress has enacted legislation that contains dire-sounding threats to agencies that do not install the FASAB system, but those threats are weak compared with the power of the purse. Managers at all levels will continue to base their decisions on the obligation data and ignore the expense-based data. Because neither accountants nor managers will pay attention to the in-formation in the expense-based accounts, the FASAB system will simply atrophy.

Agency Level. As a practical matter, it would be impossible to have two accounting systems at the level of agencies and their responsibility centers: one for obligations and the other for expenses. Accounting information is used in planning op-erations, in preparing the related budget, and in managing operations.

Budget preparation requires hours of effort during the budget season from January through the spring. At the DoD thousands of people devote many hours to making propos-als, selling those proposals at committee meetings and infor-mal meetings, countering proposals from those who are com-peting for the same dollars, forcing the numbers to come within prescribed limits, and preparing for defense at the OMB and congressional committees. They range from ser-geants to four-star generals or admirals and equivalent ranks of civilians.

Managers use the accounting amounts as an aid in making operating decisions. They would not use two sets of numbers for the same factual situation; using one set is difficult enough. In choosing between two systems, they obviously will choose the obligation system because it has the power of the purse.

An Unnecessarily Complicated System

Standards setters should limit their rules to topics that require useful information about the same set of facts. They should resist the temptation to discuss topics that are interesting but unnecessary for a system that develops useful information for managers and outside parties. In this section I describe FASAB requirements that do not meet this criterion.

Balance Sheet. The FASAB probably assumed without analysis that a balance sheet is a necessary component of any accounting system. All business systems have a balance sheet; therefore, the government should have one. This assumption is not defensible.

The two Hoover Commissions mentioned above did not recommend a balance sheet for the federal government. Neither did the report of the Ash Council in 1971, that of the Carter Reorganization Project in 1979, or the Vice President's *National Performance Review* in 1993.

Many Assets Are Omitted. The assets listed on the balance sheet are supposed to be the resources owned by the government. Actually, they constitute only a small fraction of the government's assets. They do not include the millions of acres of land used for parks and grazing. They do not include the rights to minerals beneath the surface of this land, the forests on this land, or the minerals in the continental shelf. They do not include weapons systems, space exploration equipment, monuments, or "heritage" assets (e.g., the Lee Mansion). They do not include the assets of the legislative and judicial branches. They do include the Louisiana Purchase at its $15 million cost in 1803. That land is an area about one-fourth of the total area of the United States, but $15 million today is the price of a city block.

Moreover, the federal government has resources that are far more important than business assets in judging its ability to meet its liabilities: It can levy taxes, and it can print money.

The long-lived assets reported on the FASAB balance sheet include only the items owned by agencies that carry out normal government activities. Those assets are a small fraction of total government long-lived assets, but there is no way of knowing the size of that fraction or whether the fraction of reported items from year to year is a constant proportion of the total.

The total for property, plant, and equipment assets listed in the 1999 U.S. government balance sheet is $299 billion. Property, plant, and equipment is defined by the federal government as tangible items owned by the federal government and having an expected and useful life of more than two years (Concepts Statement No. 2).

This is an extraordinarily low amount. The correct amount, if it could be found, would be in the trillions.

In 50 years of experience with accounting at the agency level, I never used a balance sheet and do not know of anyone who has.

The FASAB has not described a use for balance sheet information. Its lengthy description in the 1993 and 1995 "Federal Financial Concepts Statements" lists many uses for operating statement information, but only one sentence addresses the usefulness of the balance sheet as a whole. That sentence says that the balance sheet helps readers determine "whether the government's financial position improved or deteriorated over the period." Because it lists only a tiny, unknown fraction of the government's assets, the FASAB balance sheet does not come close to doing this.

A balance sheet for a lending agency is useful to financial analysts. Government electrical generating plants, water distribution systems, the postal service, and similar businesslike activities whose prices are based on recovering costs should prepare conventional balance sheets that include fixed assets. A report that lists *monetary* assets of the whole federal government is useful to political scientists; such a report has been prepared by the Treasury Department for many years.

The government does need a record of its assets. Agencies

must record the cost of newly acquired fixed assets; this is a necessary part of any accounting system because debits must equal credits. The system should keep track of an agency's assets. The General Services Administration, the State Department, and some other agencies have such records. All agencies should have them. Those records should be audited, but the numbers need not be aggregated into a balance sheet.

At the state and local levels the numbers for property, plant, and equipment have some meaning. These assets usually were financed by issuing bonds, and the debt service (i.e., principal and interest) on those bonds must be recovered by taxes or other sources. The amount a municipality or state government can borrow is limited by the amount of assets it owns or will own. In the federal government there is no such relationship between expenses and assets.

An accounting system is especially important for projects that require several years to complete, such as aircraft, space exploration, ships, dams, roads, and other major capital appropriations. The FASAB should add a section to its rules that accepts existing practices, that is, rules for accounting for major projects. This would be a welcome contrast to the other sections, most of which describe untried practices. It would demonstrate that the FASAB system need not break entirely new ground.

Building a useful balance sheet is no more feasible than trying to build a multistory sand castle when there is not enough sand. Children learn this, and so should the FASAB. The GAO has made many reports of the inadequacy of the accounts. The most important ones are those of the Department of Defense, the Forest Service, and the Internal Revenue Service.

The FASAB uses a considerable proportion of its available resources in discussing rules for building a balance sheet, more than on any other issue. Those documents probably involve more discussion, memorandums, and exposure drafts than does any topic actually reported on the financial statements. For example, discussion papers deal with whether a U.S. Coast Guard vessel should be treated as an agency asset or a weapons system because the vessel becomes part of the navy in wartime. Agency assets are reported on the balance sheet; weapons systems are not. The FASAB's original pronouncement on property, plant, and equipment, "Statement of Federal Financial Accounting Standards," No. 6 (SFFAS6, 1995) already has been amended twice.

A few people argue for a balance sheet on the grounds that it is necessary as a way to demonstrate that debits equal credits. This is not so. The total of the debits has no relationship whatsoever to the actual assets owned by the federal government. Because it obviously is unable to list all the assets, there is no reason for reporting that the number for total assets equals the total of liabilities plus equities.

Some may argue that the amount for assets must be correct because the auditor has not challenged it. Although the audit procedure is not clear, I am reasonably sure that no outside audit checks the validity of the amounts recorded as assets or calls attention to items that although perfectly legitimate assets are omitted from the balance sheet.

Moreover, the definition of what is included in various items changes from year to year, and that invalidates any comparison of items. For example, the expenditures by the Navy Specials Weapons Office were reported as Office of Secretary of Defense in some years, as navy in other years, and as separate appropriations in other years. This of course invalidates any comparison of those items.

Depreciation and Book Value. The FASAB rules for long-lived assets are similar to those used in business; that is, items of plant and equipment are to be reported at their original cost less depreciation. The resulting book value presumably measures the portion of the cost that so far has not been written off as an expense. Businesses have recognized depreciation ever since the amount became tax-deductible in the 1920s. Except for businesslike agencies (e.g., utilities, realtors, renters, and agencies that provide services for which they are reimbursed), few government agencies have records of the book value of their long-lived assets. Constructing those records would be a huge task.

Even if reporting book value were feasible, the numbers in most agencies would be meaningless. Book value is not what an asset could be sold for. It is not a cost that must be recovered; because the acquisition was financed by a capital appropriation, the cost to the agency was zero. It is not an amount that is pledged to meet liabilities.

In 1956, during my first appearance before a congressional committee, I took a dim view of the usefulness of a depreciation number in the planning and control of operating activities of the federal government. Forty-seven years later I feel the same way. I do not believe that this reflects mere stubbornness.

Stewardship Assets. Statement No. 8 (SFFAS8, 1997) requires a separate report, "Supplementary Stewardship Reporting." This is supposed to report the results obtained by an agency as well as the expenses it incurred. The report is divided into seven categories, each with a set of requirements. For example, the "human capital" section requires that the accomplishments of each training program offered to the public be reported and requires that actual accomplishments (including both "outputs" and "outcome") be compared with budgeted amounts. Few, if any, agencies take these requirements seriously; the task simply is not feasible. The FASAB might claim that these requirements merely flesh out the requirements of the Government Performance and Results Act of 1994; this is an unacceptable excuse for publishing a foolish standard.

Deferred Maintenance. Statement No. 6 (SFFAS6, 1995), "Accounting for Property, Plant, and Equipment," requires that the cost of deferred maintenance be reported. Conceptually, this cost is the amount that should have been but was not spent to maintain assets in good condition. This would be important information, but there is no reliable way of estimating what the amount is. Because it is a "soft" number, managers would not pay much attention to it. Including this as an FASAB standard adds to the impression that the standards setters are naïve.

Cost Accounting. Statement No. 4 (SFFAS4, 1995), "Managerial Cost Accounting Standards," is an elementary, superficial discussion of cost accounting. The Cost Accounting Standards Board has developed standards for calculating allowable costs for federal cost-type contracts. They are necessary for this purpose, and they are complicated. Most standards setters dispose of this topic with a few principles. The FASAB should do the same thing.

International Public Sector Accounting Standards (IPSASs) are being developed by the Public Sector Committee (PSC) of the International Federation of Accountants in New York. These cost accounting standards have received no authoritative support.

Suggested Actions

Experience over the last five years has demonstrated that the FASAB system is a failure. The principal reason for this failure is that government agencies are required by Congress to use two quite different and incompatible accounting systems for the management of operating activities: an obligation-based system and an expense-based system. No manager can make decisions or control performance under those circumstances.

I suggest that the FASAB statements relating to the government as a whole should be deleted. (Some of the material in No. 2, "Accounting for Direct Loans and Loan Guarantees"; No. 4, "Managerial Cost Accounting Standards"; No. 7, "Accounting for Revenue and Other Financing Sources"; and No. 10, "Accounting for Internal Use Software" may be useful in the revised material.)

The FASAB should develop a set of management accounting standards for federal agencies. Management accounting texts provide a basis for those standards.

The FASAB should focus its attention on developing a management accounting system for the use of individual federal agencies:

- The focus should be on responsibility centers, which are organization units headed by a manager who is responsible for a unit's output and the expenses incurred in arriving at that output.
- Responsibility centers relate to operating activities. Costs associated with acquiring or constructing capital assets should be recorded in separate responsibility centers. The procedures for capital responsibility centers are already adequate. Recognition of this fact should give more credence to the overall effort.
- Some responsibility centers may be an aggregate of all the responsibility centers in an agency, but this aggregation may not be feasible in certain situations. For example, I doubt that it would be feasible to treat the U.S. Army as a responsibility center.
- Expenses are the resources used by a responsibility center and the resources charged to it from other responsibility centers for the work they do.
- Expenses incurred in other responsibility centers can be charged to the consuming responsibility center through the use of working capital funds. Those funds provide a way to convert obligated amounts to consumption amounts, a procedure that is not necessary in business responsibility centers.
- The use of working capital funds to charge layers of overhead costs to responsibility centers is not worthwhile.
- Records of assets owned by the government should continue to be maintained, and overhead costs should be collected but not charged to any operating units. These records are necessary for operating purposes. Excellent records for inventory control already exist. Most agencies have some record of capital assets. The navy has a record of the cost of the *USS Constitution (Old Ironsides)*, which was commissioned in 1798. Also, agencies should have adequate records of the nature and loca-

tion of all their capital assets. This is not a requirement for aggregating them in a single balance sheet, however.

- Some responsibility centers earn revenue by delivering products to outside consumers. Others compete with civilian firms that provide the same service. If the charges made for those products includes an allowance for depreciation, the system should incorporate depreciation. Depreciation should not be used in other responsibility centers. The fixed assets for those centers are financed by capital budget items. Charging depreciation for the same items would be double counting.

- This announcement should be made immediately. Software firms and information technology departments within agencies are hard at work developing programs for the system, as required by the FASAB. I have been told that the cost of the efforts now under way will be hundreds of millions of dollars. The system developers must follow the requirements that currently exist no matter what they think about their desirability. They will welcome the opportunity to use their abilities on more productive projects.

Education

The expense-based system is the most drastic change made in federal government accounting in 50 years. The task of educating people about it will be tremendous. There are two quite different groups that must be educated: accountants and managers.

A modest education program for federal accountants is under way. It consists of conferences that use materials mostly developed by professional firms. The sessions have not been well attended because many people do not take the FASAB system seriously. These efforts consist of conferences, videos, and booklets.

The education of managers is much more important. Managers are accustomed to an obligation-based system. The closest they come to an expense-based system is in working-capital funds. They will not recognize initially that the system is much more useful in decision making and control than is the obligation system they have been using. I know of no pertinent training programs for managers.

From accounts in various publications and information furnished by educators and managers, the size of the implementation effort seems clear: It is pitiful. Much more information has been published about the relatively new consumer smart card than about the new accounting system. The winter 1999 issue of *Armed Forces Comptroller* has 18 articles about aspects of financial management systems in the DoD, but only two of them mention the FASAB system, and they focus on bookkeeping mechanics rather than on usefulness to managers (Noe, 1999; Thomas, 1999).

Unless Congress accepts an expense-based system, the work of the FASAB will be of little value.

Notes

[1] Several years ago the army overspent its obligation authority by $225 million because its control system broke down, but no one went to jail and no one was fined $225 million.

[2] My examples are taken from the Department of Defense because I am familiar with that organization. Similar examples can be found in other agencies.

[3] Although Statement 34 deals only with financial statements, the budget system is necessarily consistent with it. The financial statements of state and local governments are reported in accordance with the "rules of the game"; the budget system must be consistent with those rules.

[4] Informal, unaudited financial statements had been published by the GAO for several years prior to 1997. They were estimates derived from then currently available data.

[5] The mechanics are described in Robert N. Anthony and David W. Young, *Management Control in Nonprofit Organizations* (Burr Ridge, IL.: Irwin/McGraw-Hill, 1999), pp. 536–538.

11

SUMMARY OF RECOMMENDATIONS

This chapter summarizes the principal recommendations I have made in financial accounting rules pronounced by the three American standards-setting bodies: the Financial Accounting Standards Board (FASB) for business and nonprofit organizations, the Governmental Accounting Standards Board (GASB) for state and local governments, and the Federal Accounting Standards Advisory Board (FASAB) for the federal government.

Financial accounting standards are rules that govern the information furnished by an entity to outside parties. They exist because they are the rules users presumably would use if outside parties were able to influence them.

Chapter 3: The Financial Position Statement

The balance sheet should be superseded by a solvency statement which lists only assets whose fair value can be measured. It lists liabilities as now measured. It suggests other changes in the report of an entity's financial status.

Chapter 4: The Income Statement

The cost of using capital assets should be recognized as a cost in accounting. That cost should be recognized as the cost of relevant assets and expenses. This will eliminate a principal cause of the differences between financial accounting and economics.

Chapter 5: Statement of Changes in Equity

There should be an income statement and a separate statement of changes in owner equity; the two statements should not be mingled. This requires changes or deletions of Accounting Principles Board Opinions 12, 19, and 20 and FASB Statements 95 and 130.

Chapter 6: The Cash Flow Statement

The cash flow statement should emphasize the "indirect" method rather than the "direct" method, which it currently emphasizes.

Even though the statement is not limited to cash flows, it should be called a cash flow statement.

The operating section should be reorganized to emphasize changes in working capital.

Investing and financing activities should not be classified separately. Instead, preparers should be encouraged to report the nonoperating flows in whatever format is most informative.

Chapter 7: Nonprofit Accounting

The approach here should be similar to that used before the issuance of the FASB's rules on nonprofit organizations. In general, these rules should differ from those for other organizations only in that there should be special treatment of contributed capital. The distinction between unrestricted, temporarily restricted and permanently restricted should be superseded by a distinction between contributed capital and other items. Contributions for current use should be treated as a revenue item.

Depreciation expense on contributed plant should be recognized.

Gains and losses on contributed capital should be recognized according to current practice.

The category of "exchange" transactions should be replaced by reporting those payments as liabilities.

Pledges for the current year should be reported as a receivable. Pledges for capital purposes should not be entered in the accounts; they should be reported in a note.

"Nonreciprocal transfers" should be reported as contribution revenue.

The special terminology used in statement headings should be replaced by business terms.

Chapter 8: State and Local Government Accounting

The Governmental Accounting Standards Board has issued rules that require government organizations to prepare two complete sets of accounting information: one based on the traditional fund-accounting system and the other based on the modern accrual accounting. The two systems are both confusing and unnecessary. The material on fund accounting should be deleted.

Chapter 9: Implementation

There should be a thorough editorial review of existing standards to eliminate duplications, synonyms, illustrations, and appendixes.

A new taxonomy should be constructed that is in accordance with the beginning recommended by the XBRL Group and resulting in a rearrangement of existing standards. This is a huge effort. One possibility is that it could be undertaken by the new Public Company Accounting Oversight Board. Whatever arrangement is finally chosen, it should work closely with the International Accounting Standards Board. The committee presumably will contract for the details of this work.

The result will be one set of standards for business organizations, nonprofit organizations, and state and local governments. The first effort should be a new set of overall standards. After this is completed, special standards for certain industries should be developed.

Chapter 10: Federal Accounting Standards

There should be no federal balance sheet. The FASAB should develop a set of management accounting principles for federal agencies. It should focus on responsibility centers, resources used by responsibility centers (i.e., expenses), and working capital funds to transfer expenses from one responsibility center to another. Records of assets owned by the government should continue to be maintained, and overhead costs should be collected but not charged to any operating units.

The House Appropriations Committee should shift from its current obligation system to an expense-based system. If it is unwilling to do so, there can be no satisfactory federal accounting system for operating purposes.

REFERENCES

American Accounting Association. 1936 "A Tentative Statement of Accounting Principles Underlying Corporate Financial Statements. *The Accounting Review* (June): 187–91.

———. 1964. Concepts and Standards Research Study Committee, "The Realization Concept," *Accounting Review*. (April).

———. 1965. Concepts and Standards Research Study Committee, "The Realization Concept," *Accounting Review*. (April).

———. 1966. Committee to Prepare a Statement of Basic Accounting Theory. *A Statement of Basic Accounting Theory.*

———. 2000. Financial Accounting Standards Committee, "Reporting Financial Instruments."

American Institute of Accountants. *Changing Concepts of Business Income: Report of Study Group on Business Income.* New York: The Macmillan Company. 1952.

American Institute of Certified Public Accountants (AICPA). *Accounting Research Bulletins* 1953.

———. 1970. *APB Statement No. 4. Basic Concepts and Accounting Principles Underlying Financial Statements of Business Enterprises.*

———*Accounting Principles Board Opinions (APB).* 1962–73.

———*Accounting trends and techniques* (Annual).

———. 1973. Study Group on the Objectives of Financial Statements, Robert M. Trueblood, Chairman. *Objectives of Financial Statements.* New York: AICPA.

———. 1973. Accounting Principles Board. *Opinion No. 30: Reporting the Results of Operations—Reporting the Effects of Disposal of a Segment of a Business, and Extraordinary, Unusual and Infrequently Occurring Events and Transactions.* New York: AICPA.

———. 1988. Statement on Auditing Standards, No. 59, *The Auditor's Consideration of an Entity's Ability to Continue as a Going Concern.*

———. 1994. Special Committee on Financial Reporting. *Comprehensive Report, "Improving Business Reporting—A Customer Focus."* New York: AICPA.

Anthony, Robert. 1956. Testimony before the Senate Subcommittee on Government Operations, S. 3897, A Bill to Improve Governmental Budgeting and Accounting Methods and Procedures.

———. 1956. Hawkins, D. F., and K. A. Merchant. *Accounting: Text and Cases.* Original Title: *Management Accounting: Text and Cases.* Homewood, IL: Richard D. Irwin, Inc.

———. 1963. Showdown on Accounting Principles. *Harvard Business Review* (May–June): 99–106.

———. 1971. Closing the Loop Between Planning and Performance. *Public Administration Review* (May–June): 388–98.

———. 1977. Equity Interest: A Cure for the Double Taxation of Dividends. *Financial Executive* (July): 20–23.

———. 1978. *Financial Accounting in Nonbusiness Organizations: An Exploratory Study of Conceptual Issues.* Stamford, CT: Financial Accounting Standards Board.

———. 1979. Statement for the U.S. Senate Subcommittee on Government Efficiency, August 31. Accounting Principles.

———. 1982. Proposed Financial Accounting Standards for Nonbusiness Organizations. *HBS Working Paper 82–35.*

———. 1982. Recognizing the cost of interest on equity. *Harvard Business Review* (January–February): 91–96.

———. 1983. *Tell It Like It Was: A Conceptual Framework for Financial Accounting.* Burr Ridge, IL: Richard D. Irwin.

———. 1984. *Future Directions for Financial Accounting.* Burr Ridge, IL: Dow Jones-Irwin.

———. 1997c. "Financial Reporting in the 1990s and Beyond." *Accounting Horizons* (December).

———. 1997d. Financial Reporting in Nonprofit Organizations: A Proposal." *Harvard Business School Working Paper 93–039.* Rev. 3/97.

———. Hawkins, D. E., K. A. Merchant, 1999. *Accounting Text and Cases.* Tenth Edition. Burr Ridge, IL: Irwin/McGraw-Hill.

———. Young, D. W., 1999. *Management Control in Nonprofit Organizations*, 6th edition. Burr Ridge, IL: Irwin/McGraw-Hill.

Association for Investment Management and Research (AIMR), 1993. "Financial Reporting in the 1990s and Beyond." Charlottesville, VA: AIMR.

Barrett, M. J. et al. 1991. American Accounting Association Committee on Auditing Measurement, 1989–90. *Accounting Horizons* 5 (September): 81–105.

Barth, M. E., and W. R. Landsman. 1995. Fundamental Issues Related to Using Fair Value Accounting Reporting. *Accounting Horizons* 9 (December): pp. 97–107.

Beaver, W. H. 1987. *Financial Reporting: An Accounting Revolution.* Englewood Cliffs, NJ: Prentice-Hall.

Beckett, J. R., 1966. "The Inadequacy of Financial Accounts as Applicable to Public Companies," *Accountants' Journal*, Vol. 44, (June).

Beresford, D. R. 1999. It's time to simplify accounting standards. *Journal of Accountancy* (March): 65–67. Donald J. Kirk.

———. And L. T. Johnson. 1995. "Interactions between the FASB and the Academic Community." *Accounting Horizons* (December): 108–17.

———. L. T. Johnson and C. L. Retiher. 1996. "Is a Second Income Statement Needed?" *Journal of Accountancy* (April): 69–72.

Best, A. M., 1999 "Insolvency: Will Historic Trends Return?" *Best's Review* (March).

Black's Law Dictionary, 1990. Sixth edition. West Publishing Co.

Brief, R. J. 1993. *The Continuing Debate over Depreciation, Capital and Income*, Garland Publishing, Inc.

Brockholdt, J. L. 1978. "Influence of Nineteenth and Early Twentieth Century Railroad Accounting on Development of Modern Accounting Theory," *The Accounting Historians Journal*, (Spring).

Brookings Institution and the American Enterprise Institute. 2000. *The GAAP Gap: Corporate Disclosure in the Internet Age*. (March).

Buckeley, W. M., and Mark Maremont "Xerox Replaces Auditor KPMG Amid Tension." *Wall Street Journal* (October 8, 2001).

Castellano, James G. "Restoring Public Confidence." *Journal of Accountancy* (April 2002).

Chatfield, M. 1977. *A History of Accounting Thought*. Huntington, New York: Robert E. Krieger Publishing Company.

———. and R. Vangermeersch, 1966. *The History of Accountancy: An Encyclopedia*, LC 95-20710, Reference Library of the Humanities Ser.: Vol. 1573.

Comptroller General of the United States. (Annual) "Report on Consolidated Financial Statements." March 31, 1999.

Conant, S., and N. L. Desoutter, D. L. Long, and R. MacGrogan, 1996. *Managing for Solvency and Profitability in Life and Health Insurance Companies*, Life Office Management Association, Inc. (LOMA), 1996.

Craig, Susanne, and J. Weil "Despite Losses, Complex Deals Analysts Remain High on Enron." *Wall Street Journal*, (October 26, 2001).

Dean, Joel, 1951. *Capital Budgeting*. New York. Columbia University Press.

Derieux, S. A. 2000. Let's Reassess Accounting Standards. *Journal of Accountancy*. (March) 82–83.

Dyckman, T. R., and S. A. Zeff. 1984. Two decades of the "Journal of Accounting Research." *Journal of Accounting Research* 22 (Spring): 225–297.

Edey, H. C., and P. Panitpakdi, 1956. "British Company Accounting and the Law 1844–1900," In Littleton and Yamey (eds), *B.S. Studies in the History of British Accounting*, Sweet and Maxwell Limited.

Edwards, J. R. 1989. *A History of Financial Accounting*. London and New York: Routledge.

Federal Accounting Standards Advisory Board. 1993. "Statement of Federal Financial Accounting Concepts No. 1: Objectives of Federal Financial Reporting."

———. 1995. Statement of Federal Financial Accounting Concepts No. 2: "Entity and Display." 1995.

———. 1995. Statement of Federal Financial Accounting Standards No. 4: "Managerial Cost Accounting Standards."

———. 1995. Statement of Federal Financial Accounting Standards No. 6: "Accounting for Property, Plant, and Equipment."

———. 1997. Statement of Federal Financial Accounting Standards No. 8: "Supplementary Stewardship Reporting."

Financial Accounting Standards Board. *Current Text: Accounting Standards*. Vol 1.

———. 1996. Recommendations of the AICPA Special Committee on Financial Reporting and the Association for Investment Management and Research.

———. 1977. *Statement of financial Accounting Standards*.

Statement of Financial Accounting Concepts No. 1.

————. 1998. FASB Steering Committee, Business Reporting research Project, *Improving Business Reporting: Insights into Enhancing Voluntary Disclosure."*

————. 1999. *Original Pronouncements: Accounting Standards.* Vol 1.

————. 2000. Business Reporting Research Project. *Electronic Distribution of Business Reporting Information.*

————. 2002. Financial Accounting Series. *FASB Focuses on Three New Projects—Revenue and Liability Recognition, Disclosure about Intangible Assets, and Codification and Simplification of Accounting Literature.* (February 28).

Financial Executives International. 2002. FEI Observations and Recommendations. *Improving Financial Management, Financial Reporting and Corporate Governance.* March.

Financial Executives Research Foundation, Inc. 2001. *Quantitative Measure of the Quality of Financial Reporting* (June).

————. 2002. Financial Reporting Complexity. *Survey Looks for Solutions.* (January).

Fischer, M. 1997. Two accounting standards: One industry. *Journal of Budgeting, Accounting and Financial Management* (Summer): 251–284.

Gibson, J. *Earnings Book Value and Dividends in Security Valuation* in Aberhannell and Bernard "is the U.S. Stock Market Myopic?" University of Michigan Working Paper. 1994.

Gore, Al. 1993. "Creating A Government That Works better & Costs Less." *Report of the National Performance Review."* U.S. Government Printing Office, Washington, D.C.

Hammond, Donald V., 1999. "Testimony Before a Subcommittee of the House Government Reform Committee." (March 31).

Heath, L. C., 1978. *Financial Reporting and the Evaluation of Solvency,* AICPA.

Hirst, D. Eric, and P. Hopkins 1999. Comprehensive Income Reporting and Analysts' Valuation Judgments. *Journal of Accounting Research.* Vol 36. 47–75.

Horngren, C. T. 1973. The marketing of accounting standards. *The Journal of Accountancy* (October): 61–66.

————. 1981. Uses and limitations of a conceptual framework. *Journal of Accountancy* (April): 86–95.

International Accounting Standards Committee. 1995. *International Accounting Standards. London: IASC.*

International Federation of Accountants. 2001. *International Public Sector Accounting Standards* (IPSAS). IPSAS 1 *Presentation of Financial Statements.* (2000).

Iriji, Y. 1983. On the accountability-based conceptual framework of accounting. *Journal of Accounting and Public Policy* 2 (June): 75–81.

Johnson, L. T., Reither, C. L., and R. J. Swieringa. 1995. Toward Reporting Comprehensive Income. *Accounting Horizons.* 9-4: 128–37.

————. 1995. And C. L. Reither. "Reporting Comprehensive Income." *Financial Accounting Series—FASB Viewpoints,* no. 115-A (November): Norwalk, Conn.: FASB.

Kelly-Newton, L. 1980. *Accounting Policy Formulation: The Role of Corporate Management.* Addison-Wesley Publishing Company.

Leadbeater, Charles, 2000. Institute of Chartered Accountants in England and Wales. *New Measures for the New Economy.*

Lev, Baruch, and Paul Zarowin, (unpublished, 1999). The Boundaries of Financial Reporting and How to Extend Them. February.

Levitt, A. 2000 "Renewing the Covenant with Investors." Speech at the New York University Center for Law and Business. (May)

Loftus, J. A., and M. C. Miller, 2000. *Reporting on Solvency and Cash Position*, Australian Accounting Research Foundation.

Marks, Barry R., and K. K. Raman, 1996. "The Behavior of Interperiod Equity-Related Performance Measures Over Time." *Accounting Horizons* (December). 52–66.

Mason, A. K., and Michael Gibbins. 1991. Judgment and U.S. Accounting Standards. *Accounting Horizons*. 5 (June): 220–38.

McLean, Robert I.G, 1995. Canadian Institute of Chartered Accountants. Iperformance Measures in the New Economy. Toronto.

Monson, Dennis W., 2001. "The Conceptual Framework and Accounting for Leases." *Accounting Horizons*, (September): 277.

Montgomery, Robert H. 1912. *Accounting Theory and Practice*. New York: Ronald Press.

Mosher, Frederick C. 1979. *The GAO: The Quest for Accountability in American Government*. Boulder, CO: Westview Press, 1979.

Most, K. S. 1993. *The Future of the Accounting Profession: A Global Perspective*. Westport, CT: Quorum Books.

———. 1986. *Accounting Theory*. 2d ed. Toronto: Holt, Rinehart and Winston of Canada.

National Conference of Commissioners on Uniform State Laws, 1984. *Uniform Fraudulent Transfer Act*.

Newberry, S. 1995. Accounting for contributed services: The FASB's conceptual confusion. *Financial Accountability and Management* 11 (August): 242–258.

Noe, Kathleen. 1999. "DoD's Future Integrated Financial Systems Architecture." *Armed Forces Comptroller*. (Winter), 18–19.

Paton, W. A., and A. C. Littleton. 1940. *An Introduction to Corporate Accounting Standards*. Sarasota, FL. American Accounting Association.

———. 1922. *Accounting Theory*. New York: Ronald Press.

Previts, G. J., and B. D. Merino. 1998. *A History of Accountancy in the United States*. Ohio State University.

Riahi-Belkaoui, A., 1989. *The Coming Crisis in Accounting*, Quorum Books.

Saliars, E. A., *Accountants Handbook*, Ronald Press.

Robinson-Marc. 1998. *Measuring Compliance with the Golden Rule*. Fiscal Studies. (November): 447–462.

Schipper, K. "Commentary on Earnings Management." *Accounting Horizons* (December): 91–102.

Schroeder, M. "SEC Fines Arthur Andersen in Fraud Case; Firm to Pay $7 Million in Relation to Audits of Waste Management." *The Wall Street Journal* (June 20, 2001).

Scovell, Clinton H. 1924. *Interest As A Cost*. New York. Ronald Press.

Securities and Exchange Commission, Task Force: *Strengthening Financial Markets: Do Investors Have the Information They Need?* May 2001.

Smith, R. G., Freeman, R. J. 1996. Statement of Cash Flows: the direct vs. indirect method debate continues. *Government Finance Review*. (Feb): 17.

Solomons, D. 1978. The Politicization of Accounting, *Journal of Accountancy*. (November) 65–72.

———. 1989. *Guidelines for Financial Reporting Standards*. London. Research Board of the Institute of Chartered Accountants in England and Wales.

————. 1995. Criteria for Choosing an Accounting Model. *Accounting Horizons*. 9, 1 (March): 42–51.

Sprouse, R. T. 1971. The Balance Sheet: Embodiment of the Most Fundamental Element of Accounting Theory. In Williard E. Stone, ed. *Foundations of Accounting Theory*. Gainesville: University of Florida Press.

Sterling, R. R. 1967. A statement of basic accounting theory: A review article. *Journal of Accounting Research* (March): 95–112.

Stewart, G. B. 1994. EVA: Fact and Fantasy. *Journal of Applied Corporate Finance*. Summer. 71–84.

Storey, R. K., and S. Storey. 1998. Special report: The Framework of financial accounting concepts and standards FASB.

Sumariwalla, R. D., and W. C. Levis, 2000. *Unified Financial Reporting System for Not-for-Profit Organizations: A Comprehensive Guide to Unifying GAAP, IRS Form 990, and Other Financial Reports Using a Unified Chart of Accounts*. San Francisco, California, Jossey-Bass Inc., Publishers A. Wiley Company.

Thomas, Gerald W. 1999. "DoD's Critical Feeder Systems: Achieving Compliance with the Federal Financial Management Improvement Act of 1996." *Armed Forces Comptroller*. (Winter), 15–17.

U.S. Department of the Treasury. 1999. "1998 Consolidated Financial Statements of the Federal Government." U.S. General Accounting Office.

U.S. General Accounting Office, 2000. GAO-AIMD-00-57, "Accrual Budgeting Experiences of Other Nations and Implications for the United States." (February).

Vangermeersch, R. G., 1979. *Financial Reporting Techniques in 20 Industrial Companies Since 1861*. LC 79-1238. University of Florida Accounting Ser.: No. 9, 1110.

Van Riper, R. 1994. *Setting Standards for Financial Reporting*. Westport, CT: Quorum Books.

Walker, R. G., F. L. Clarke and G. W. Dean, 2000. "Options for Infrastructure Reporting," *Abacus*, Vol 36, No. 2.

Watts, R. L., and J. L. Zimmerman. 1978. Towards a Positive Theory of the Determination of Accounting Standards. *The Accounting Review* (January): 112–134.

Weygandt, J. J., and D. J. Noll. 1997. Business Reporting: What Comes Next. *Journal of Accountancy* (February) 59.

Whittington, G., 1971. *The Prediction of Profitability and Other Studies of Company Behavior*, Cambridge University Press.

XBRL International. "Progress Report." April 2003.

Zeff, S. A. 1986. Big eight firms and the accounting literature: The falloff in advocacy writing. *Journal of Accounting, Auditing and Finance* 1 (2): 131–154.

————. 1995. A Perspective on the U.S. Public/Private Sector Approach to the Regulation of Financial reporting. *Accounting Horizons* (March).

————. 1999. The Evolution of The Conceptual Framework for Business Enterprises in the United States. *Accounting Historians Journal* (December): 88–131.

Zeff, S. A., and Bala and Dharon. 1997. Readings and Notes on Financial Accounting. 5th Edition. New York: Irwin McGraw-Hill

Zwieg, P., and D. Foust. 1997. Corporate America is fed up with FASB. *Business Week* (April): 108–110.

Robert N. Anthony is Ross Graham Walker Professor of Management Control Emeritus at Harvard Business School. He has been directly involved in the development of financial accounting standards for 30 years.

He is the author or co-author of 27 books, with more than two million copies in print. They have been translated into 13 languages. He is the author or co-author of over 100 articles.

In the 1970s he was a member of the committee that was established to develop principles for the new Financial Accounting Standards Board that superceded the Accounting Principles Board.

In 1978 he published a report *Financial Accounting in Non-business Organizations*. This led to the formation of a committee on non-business organizations, of which he was chairman.

This committee had over 50 members representing the then accounting standards for the several separate types of nonprofit organizations. This committee worked and held meetings in several cities.

As assistant Secretary of Defense, Comptroller from 1965 to 1968, he was responsible for developing and implementing new financial accounting standards for the Department of Defense, the largest government agency.

He worked for several states developing new financial accounting systems. He was chairman of the committee set up to revise the accounting system of the State of New York in 1979-85. He was a member of the committee appointed by the General Accounting Office to audit financial statements of New York City, 1977-85.

He has served on committees of, or as a consultant to, the National Research Council, President's Private Sector Survey on Cost Control, Federal Judicial Center, Federal Trade Commission, Price Commission in the Executive Office of the President, and other federal, state, and municipal government agencies.

He was a consultant to the Cost Accounting Standards Board, 1971-80. He participated in the development of cost accounting principles for this Board.

Throughout this period he was a member of the U.S. General Accounting Office, Educator Consultant Panel, 1973-87.

He has been a director of Warnaco, Inc., Carborundum Company, and Continental Oil Company. He was trustee of Colby College (including chairman of the Board) and Dartmouth Hitchcock Medical Center.

He was a consultant to 11 other government organizations.

He was an expert witness in representing litigation by Eastman Kodak Company, TransAlaskan Pipeline, Corn Wet Milling Industry, and the United Shoe Machinery Corporation. He has testified before several Congressional committees.